HOST YOUR OWN TV SHOW

FIVE STEPS TO HELP YOU BECOME A TOP TV PERSONALITY

TIM TIALDO

WestBow
PRESS
A DIVISION OF THOMAS NELSON

WestBow Press books may be ordered through booksellers or by contacting:

WestBow Press
A Division of Thomas Nelson
1663 Liberty Drive
Bloomington, IN 47403
www.westbowpress.com
1-(866) 928-1240

Because of the dynamic nature of the Internet, any web addresses or links contained in this book may have changed since publication and may no longer be valid. The views expressed in this work are solely those of the author and do not necessarily reflect the views of the publisher, and the publisher hereby disclaims any responsibility for them.

Any people depicted in stock imagery provided by Thinkstock are models, and such images are being used for illustrative purposes only.

Certain stock imagery © Thinkstock.

ISBN: 978-1-4497-7172-0 (hc)
ISBN: 978-1-4497-7173-7 (sc)
ISBN: 978-1-4497-7174-4 (e)

Library of Congress Control Number: 2012919629

Printed in the United States of America

WestBow Press rev. date: 10/29/2012

Table of Contents

Acknowledgements

This book is dedicated to the many people who have had such a positive impact on my life over the years. Thank you to my family, who've always instilled confidence and belief in me and supported me every step of the way. Mom, you've always shown me through example how to dig deep when things got tough and I have never forgotten that. Dad, you've always been a source of strength and love and I have become the man I am today because of you. To the many friends who've given me encouragement, support and guidance, you are wonderful. To my inner circle of positive, inspiring, encouraging and amazing best friends, you know who you are and you're all awesome human beings! To the many hosts and colleagues who inspired me, mentored me and taught me how to navigate the Television business. To Heather, you're simply amazing and give me the greatest joy in my life; I'm blessed and lucky to have you! A big thanks to all of you who have chosen to read this book and better yourselves by acquiring more knowledge. And most of all, I give thanks to my Lord and Savior Jesus Christ, who has given me the strength, talents, knowledge, understanding and ability to focus on helping others through the gifts he has instilled in me.

Special Thanks to the Following Contributors Who Made
This Book Possible

Maureen Browne	Lisa Ritter
Kim Parrish	Bucky Bowman
Kristi Capel	Brian Tracy
Shanna Hilt	Marc Cashman
Paul Cook	Clarissa French
Nikki Boyer	Karl Krummenacher
Brian Rose	Sean Sortor
Mark Turner	Nicole Wilkins
Shandi Finnessey	Rick & Lynn Hensel
Todd Newton	Jon Lineback

Introduction

When I started in working in TV in 2000, two reality shows existed, *Survivor* and *Who Wants to Marry a Millionaire?* I worked at *Access Hollywood* at the time, so I had the chance to see the inner workings of these shows from a unique perspective. Apparently nobody cared if anybody wanted to marry a millionaire because it only lasted a short time and has been called one of the 25 worst shows of all time by *TV Guide*. *Survivor*, on the other hand, became a cultural icon and ratings giant for CBS. Somehow, the show has made it 12 years and continues to get solid ratings. Those two shows changed the face of television forever and started what we now know as the "reality television craze."

A newspaper journalist with the Tampa Bay Times explained this craze well:

"Television's need for quick, shocking, cheap programming met young audiences' needs for a new form and media technology's new ability to make the personal public. Put more simply, low-rated cable channels and financially squeezed TV networks needed low cost programming that could hold the young viewers that advertisers love. As that audience got bored with scripted situation comedies, the demand for something that seemed more unpredictable and genuine led to a world where watching a man claim to pick his fiancée on national television seemed not only reasonable, but fairly entertaining."

Even though the two pioneer shows were referred to as "unscripted reality," the one and only commonality they shared was that both formats required a host: Jay Thomas for *Who Wants to Marry a Millionaire* and Jeff Probst for *Survivor*. Two very different jobs, but both required the unique energy and passion to connect with an audience. So, not only was a new genre of television being born, but an industry that previously only sourced a few jobs, most of which were very difficult to land, now had a revolution on its hands! The world of hosting was about to become HUGE!

Since then, over 700 reality shows have aired; that's nearly 60 new unscripted shows a year! Today you no longer need to have a household name or stellar resume to host a show, you simply need to be entertaining and have the unique ability to connect with your audience. Factor in the rise of technology and you'll find that every one of us is a potential "brand." In just minutes, you can post a video on YouTube or build a Facebook page that catches the world's attention. This change has literally opened up hundreds of new doors for those already working in TV, and even those who don't, to pursue their dream of being a host!

While the opportunities to host have increased, unfortunately, so has the interest of every Tom, Dick and Harry just wanting to be on television. Whether you like it or not, that's the world we now live in. Education and experience can easily be trumped by personality and connectivity with a specific audience. As hosts and potential hosts, what we must realize is that the world of TV is not about a set of rules and standards anymore; it's about what you personally bring to the table that can turn a show concept into a "ratings getter." This is why casting directors often ask the question, 'Why would I want to watch you?"

As an example, take Mike Rowe and his show *Dirty Jobs*. When the show began, it was a pretty unique new idea to profile blue collar America, but let's be honest, most people watch the show because Mike Rowe is an amazing and entertaining host. His dry humor, great personality and ability to improvise make

Dirty Jobs a must-watch for millions of people. As a result, he has become his own brand. Lee Jeans and the Ford Motor Company invested millions of dollars in making him their spokesperson. Why? Because Mike connects with their demographic, the rough, tough, roll-up-your-sleeves Americans that still believe in good old-fashioned hard work.

You may be asking yourself, "So what does this mean for me?" Well, it means three things.

- First, just about anyone with a BIG personality can be a host these days, and many people just like you have the ability to land a hosting job.
- Second, if you know how the casting world works and how to get in the right doors, you can compete and audition for the same hosting jobs that big-name current reality stars are trying to land.
- Third, the Internet has spawned an entirely new generation of hosts, the type that don't need casting directors or producers to tell them whether they've got the chops to "make it" in the business

Over the last 12 years, I've experienced some incredible highs and lows in the TV hosting business. In that time I gained a vast knowledge of the industry as I worked almost every form of entertainment media there is. I've hosted TV shows and commercials, emceed professional sporting events, pageants, even hosted training videos for large corporations. I've worked with agents, agencies and top production companies. I've even created and produced my own shows. I found myself doing any and every job that was available in the hopes that one day I would find the right fit for my personality and talents. And even though the road has honestly been hell at times, if I could do it all over again, I wouldn't do it any other way. Being a host is so much more than a career, it's a part of your soul that, if tapped in to, carries you to greater heights than you could ever imagine. Game Show Host Todd Newton summed up the hosting industry incredibly well:

"The entertainment industry is reserved for those of us who know in our hearts that we would fail miserably in a 9-to-5 environment. We seek thrills and take risks that others label foolish. We are the dreamers that live by ratings and second season pickups. While most people consider a year to consist of 365 days, ours is only 13 weeks ... and we love it that way. We all want that full-time hosting gig where we can travel the world, meet the most amazing people and have access to places, things and opportunities that we never would have seen had we not had a camera crew in tow. It is and will continue to be a fascinating journey ... and we do it as ourselves and not what people tell us we need to or should be. I am a host."

If this sounds like the life you want to pursue, then keep reading! Hosting is all about having a personality that exudes an inordinate amount of energy and excitement, and the ability to talk and present in a way most others dream about. If you think you have the gift, I highly encourage you to pursue becoming a host because you will NOT be disappointed!

The great news is that the world of hosting has drastically changed over the past decade. There are many different genres you can host shows in. There are shopping hosts, game show hosts, web TV hosts, lifestyle show hosts and reality show hosts, not to mention hosts for the big entertainment journalism shows like *Access Hollywood* and *Entertainment Tonight.* In addition, now there's YouTube and Facebook to help broadcast yourself through social media. And technology is so much easier to operate and more affordable than ever before. There are now tiny, affordable HD cameras and editing equipment that make it easy to get yourself out there and be in front of a camera doing what you love! I've seen 8 year olds edit their own video in Imovie, so the excuses to not do this yourself are few and far between!

But what I and many other hosts in the business have noticed over the past few years is there isn't one really good resource to tell you how to get into hosting, what to expect and how to develop your talents. Sure, there's always the die-hard advice you get from industry gurus who tell you that without moving to L.A. or New York, you don't have a prayer. But I've personally overcome that stereotypical B.S. The whole point of this book is to give you a step-by-step framework of how anyone with the drive and determination, can become a host, no matter where you're from or where you currently live.

This book will teach you five central themes about the TV hosting biz:

1) What is a Host? – The term "host" is thrown around very loosely these days. There are seven classic attributes that not only make a great host, but also constitute what today's casting directors and producers are seeking. You'll also learn best ways to mentally prepare yourself for the journey ahead.

2) Developing Your Talent – You'll learn in-depth explanations of the various types of hosting jobs available today. Which job a prospective host chooses will greatly determine what kind of education and skill set they need to focus on. There are multiple ways to prepare to become a host. Options include coaches, workshops, classes, courses and personal exercises. I explain each and give my personal recommendations.

3) Marketing and Branding Yourself – This is easily the No. 1 area in which most hosts or want-to-be hosts lack education. You'll get a detailed description on how to develop your personal brand and market yourself in today's media environment. I'll also give step-by-step instructions on how to develop the host's calling cards:

   • The Demo Reel

- Resume
- Biography
- Headshot

Without these, you will have a difficult time breaking into the business as a host. There's a lot of misguided information out there on what content should go into each of these calling cards. By the end of this section, I'll make sure you know exactly how to create them and what content is most effective. I'll then explain the best ways to generate a fan base, get noticed and build a strong following through social media. You'll receive step-by step instructions on how to properly build your social media marketing tools.

4) Working with an Agent – Many people ask, "Do I need an agent?" It's a very good question to ask, and, unfortunately, there is no one right answer for everyone. It all depends on the prospective host's goals, personal situation and a range of other factors. In this section we'll walk through:

- What an agent does
- How they get paid
- What they look for in a potential client
- What to look for in an agent
- The correct way to seek out an agent

Then we'll explore how to go it on your own without and agent and what that requires. By the end of this chapter, you will be able to determine if an agent is right for you.

5) The Audition Process – The audition is the one step that ALL hosts wanting to be on network television will go through. This can be nerve-wracking, embarrassing and stressful if you don't understand how to properly prepare for it. I'll take you through the different types of auditions;

walk through each step of the process, and offer insight and advice from some of today's top casting directors.

Over my years in TV, I've come to know and befriend some of the greatest coaches, producers, casting directors and hosts on the air today. Combined with their knowledge and experience, this book is an effort to make the hosting world more accessible and understandable to those wanting to pursue a career in it. There is a lot of false information out there that you have to fit a certain stereotype to be considered a great host. I'm here to tell you there is nothing further from the truth. The hosting industry has been a mystery to many for too long. This book will allow you to see the amazing experience that being a host can be and how you can become the next great personality that audiences tune into watch! Get ready to learn how to host your own TV show!

Chapter 1

THE 7 ATTRIBUTES OF GREAT HOSTS

I think that my biggest attribute to any success that I have had is hard work. There really is no substitute for working hard. – Maria Bartiromo

In my teens, I had this strange fascination for "entertainment" television. Now that I look back, maybe I wasn't so strange for watching *E! News Live*, *Entertainment Tonight* and *Access Hollywood* as much as I did. Somehow these programs resonated with me in a way that nothing else on TV could. It wasn't until my college years that I learned the reason why. You see, I was never a good student in school and struggled in most of my classes. Even though my grades didn't reflect it, I always knew I was an intelligent person with a strong work ethic and deep passion. It drove me nuts that I never could do as well on tests as I thought I should have. Ironically, this led me to research and study the various human learning styles and how they affect our ability to obtain and retain knowledge:

- Visual (spatial): You prefer using pictures, images, and spatial understanding.
- Aural (auditory-musical): You prefer using sound and music.

- Verbal (linguistic): You prefer using words, both in speech and writing.
- Physical (kinesthetic): You prefer using your body, hands and sense of touch.
- Logical (mathematical): You prefer using logic, reasoning and systems.
- Social (interpersonal): You prefer to learn in groups or with other people.
- Solitary (intrapersonal): You prefer to work alone and use self-study.

As I looked this list over, I began to break down the areas of my life that I enjoyed and those I didn't. Not surprisingly, what I found is that my "likes" were audiences, TV, music and, as much as I didn't want to admit it, being the center of attention. My guess is many of you can relate to this feeling. The type of attention I attract is something that's wired into my personality. In social situations, I always seemed to draw people in and frequently found myself in the middle of the action. As I looked at the learning styles, I began to see that I wasn't abnormal; I just had a different learning style. The truth is we all have a mix of learning styles and mine heavily favored the visual, aural, physical and social styles. It's really no surprise that my learning styles were never engaged by textbooks and homework assignments. That type of learning heavily favors the verbal, logical and solitary styles. What I did find out about myself is that I love visual learning more than any other. You can show me a video, show or documentary on a subject and I can pick up in an hour what would have taken 2 or 3 weeks via the traditional textbook or class.

When I learned this information, it was a real moment of healing and relief for me. I realized the personality I was born with, the same one that made me into the person I am today, was never "below average," it simply wasn't being utilized correctly.

If you're reading this book, my guess is your learning styles may be somewhat similar to mine. That's not to say if you have one of the other learning styles you can't be a host. All I'm saying is it's likely that one of, if not all of, the four styles is part of your personal learning repertoire. The good news is that puts your personality in a category that will likely thrive and succeed in the hosting biz. As you will find throughout this book, "personality" is what a host MUST have. Without it, you'll be fighting tremendous uphill battles each and every day.

Think about when you watch a host-driven TV show. You begin to understand why personality is not only important, but vital to the success of a show and the audience's desire to watch it. We all have our favorite hosts to watch. For some it's Ryan Seacrest, for others it's Ellen Degeneres or Oprah Winfrey, or maybe it's one of the many cable TV hosts out there. Whoever it is for you, there's a reason you love to watch that person. Something about their personality resonates with you, and it's likely that you've begun to model your own style and personality after that person. For me, it's a combination of 3 hosts. I love Ty Pennington's energy, Mike Rowe's dry humor and quick wit, and the poise and professionalism of my former co-worker and mentor Nancy O' Dell.

Don't be afraid to mimic other hosts out there. They've likely taken years to mold their presentation into what it is today, and they've probably mimicked others to do so. Using others' examples as a guide to developing your style is perfectly normal. Understand that everything about the way you conduct yourself is what will either make you a host, or just another wanna-be host. Your ability to be happy, energetic, confident, excitable and compelling is the key to making you great at this job.

So, as we get started on this journey to becoming a host, or for many of you, becoming a BETTER host, I think it's very important that we have a crystal clear focus on this particular industry and exactly what a "Host" is.

What Hosts Do For a Show

Simply put, a host guides a show, program or episode on TV or on the Internet. Your job as a host will take on a variety of responsibilities depending on the type of hosting role you're in. These include narrating, interviewing, moderating and in most cases being the audience's "tour guide" and piloting the show. Many times you'll find yourself providing explanations to various situations and giving viewers information on what your show is about. What gets an audience's attention and loyalty is when you unleash that special energy and personality you were born with.

The 7 Attributes of a Great Host

You might be asking yourself, "Am I the type of personality cut out to do this?" The greatest thing about being a host today is that you don't necessarily have to have a television background to do it, just a BIG personality! And I've identified seven common attributes that just about every great host out there has.

What I'd like you to do is write down these seven attributes. When you're done, take an honest assessment of your own abilities in each of these areas. This is a great starting point from which to move forward and it will also help you to be honest with yourself on where you may need to improve. We all need direction and coaching to get better, and we can ALWAYS improve on our current skill set! That being said, here are the seven attributes that make a truly great host:

1. **You have to be confident at being YOU**. If you're not comfortable in your own skin, audiences have this unique ability to see right through you, into your soul, and they know right off the bat whether you are or are NOT confident in yourself. I think one of the very best hosts doing this over the past 20 years is Oprah Winfrey. At one time or another, all of us have likely seen Oprah. She's a cultural icon and

the most powerful host on television today! If you want to know why she has been able to attract the audience and ratings she has, it's because, despite great odds, she became incredibly comfortable and confident at being herself. Everything about her demeanor, body language, vocal tones and general ease talking to the camera says, "This is probably what she's like in person."

But it wasn't always that way. I once read an interview with Oprah where she candidly spoke about her early career struggles. Before she was ever a host, she spent time as a news anchor in Baltimore, MD. In the interview she recalled one evening when she went to a heavyweight boxing match to see Mike Tyson fight. Just before the match began, the ring announcer introduced the heavyweight champ at 220 pounds. The only thing that Oprah heard was "220 pounds," because at that time she was 220 pounds! If you've followed Oprah over the years, you know that she, like many, has always battled her weight. As you can imagine, this tends to have a negative effect on your self-esteem and confidence levels. But what Oprah told herself and what you must tell yourself is that no matter what the outside world thinks of you, you must see yourself as the person you know you are on the inside. You must believe that everyone wants to watch you and likes to watch you. When it comes down to it, that's the ultimate litmus test; if you're as confident and comfortable on camera as you are in person, you've achieved the ideal comfort level for an audience to not only watch you, but also to connect with you and WANT to tune in to see you.

2. **You must have a passion to connect with others**.
    Simply put, you HAVE TO be interested in other people! The most important thing you must learn to become a good host is that it's NOT about you or the copy (depending on

what type of show you're on); it's about the audience. If you use the word "I" often, that's likely a good indicator that you need to focus more on the "we" or "us" mentality. Think about how Apple has created and branded all of their products in the last decade. The Imac, Ipod, Ipad. These are meant to be used by "one" person. However, as a host you are talking to an audience, which means there are multiple people involved in the conversation. "I" needs to be thrown out of your vocabulary most of the time. You'll learn later in the book that this also goes for marketing yourself. Certainly there will be times when the use of "I" is completely acceptable, but if you're in this for self-glorification, if you just want to be famous, or popular or the next cast member on a reality show, the audience is going to see right through you and your hosting career will be short-lived. So, make sure that you know deep down that you have a definite interest in other people. This is incredibly important and crucial to your success as a host.

3. **You must have an outgoing personality** - I've seen the term HOST thrown around very loosely, especially by local news stations hiring for what they call "lifestyle" shows. TV news anchoring, however, is not hosting. Hosting is something that you either have the personality for or you don't. It's hard to teach charisma. The best hosts are the ones who are most comfortable in their own skin. Take Ty Pennington for example; if you ever watched *Extreme Home Makeover*, you know Ty could care less about what people think of his crazy antics. How about Kelly Ripa? She's crazy, goofy and great all at the same time! If you watched her, you'd think, "There's no way you could call what she does 'work'!" Or Adam Richman of *Man vs. Food*. I mean, really? Not only does he go out and eat himself into a coma every week, he makes it look like fun!

Like Ty, Kelly and Adam, some people just have that outgoing personality; they love being around a crowd and entertaining other people. That's why people that attract an audience are called "celebrities," because others celebrate their personality. And as I've mentioned already, that, in essence, is what hosting is! You're an entertainer and so you must act like one, whether that comes naturally or not.

4. **<u>Great improv skills</u>** – Much of what we do as hosts is completely off the cuff, and many times those priceless moments that end up causing people to come back and watch our shows again and again is our ability to react in fun and humorous ways to various situations. Watch a Tom Bergeron, Ellen Degeneres or Wayne Brady. They all have the unique ability to deliver great one-liners because of their improvisation skills. Unlike some of the other attributes, this definitely IS something that some people are born with, but that's not to say you can't learn it. There are many different improv classes out there to help you to be quick-witted on your feet. Also, I highly encourage you to watch comedians that make you laugh. You'd be amazed at what you can pick up by watching them! Growing up, I was always a big fan of Eddie Murphy, Kevin James and a host of other comedians that I would frequently watch and study. Observing my personality now, I can see that many of the nuances those comedians used in their stand-up routines have become a part of my humor and personality. You can do the same. The people that have you bursting into tears with laughter are likely the people who will best fit your personality mold. In Chapter 3, I'll recommend some good coaches you can go to for help in this area.

5. **<u>The ability to listen</u>** – Listening is not just an attribute for being a great host; it's a great attribute for life in general.

If you sit down with someone for an hour, ask questions and let them talk about themselves the entire time, they're going to walk away from that going "Man, I really enjoyed talking to that person!" But what they likely don't realize is they did ALL the talking! People, including you and me, love to hear and talk about ourselves. It's not arrogance; it's general human nature. Everyone you interact with in life and on-camera will respond best if you learn to listen to what they want to talk about and work that into your conversation. As a host, it's your job to take control of the situation and be the pilot of the show. However, if you make the people involved feel better about themselves and their time with you, it's going to make your job not only easier, but more fun and engaging for the audience.

If you want a more detailed approach as to how to deal with just about every type of personality, I highly recommend the book "*How to Win Friends and Influence People*" by Dale Carnegie. It's one of my favorite books of all time, and it will teach you how to become a great conversationalist and develop relationships quickly and with ease.

6. **Be able to market yourself!**
This is easily the most underdeveloped and mysterious attribute the hosting world struggles with. The whole hosting landscape has changed so much over the past decade. It's not about just about being an "OK" host anymore. You need to have the right tools and be able to develop your own brand. And with social media and Internet resources, it's a lot easier to build your brand because hosts can literally create their own opportunities by taping video blogs and webisodes every day. You can do this anywhere and anytime and with minimal investment. In chapters 7 & 8, I'm going to go over how you can market yourself as a host and provide you with some amazing FREE resources you can take advantage

of. If you do, you'll better your chances of getting a call back or even getting the job! So, keep reading!

7. **<u>A Thick Skin</u>**

It's definitely an unfortunate reality of the business we work in, but in order to be successful in the entertainment industry, one of the most difficult things you'll have to overcome is rejection. You have to have a strong sense of who you are; otherwise you won't last long. Remember, there are hundreds of people auditioning for each hosting gig out there. For every person that lands the job, there are hundreds of others that don't, and somewhere along the line you will be one of them. Knowing this ahead of time, you must develop patience, and if you don't, you're going to add a ton of unneeded stress to your life and the lives of those around you. As a caveat to that, let me give you some insider advice. There are many people in this industry that try to avoid rejection by cutting corners and "manipulating" the situation. These people NEVER succeed and tend to burn many bridges in the process. Stay true to who you are. If you go to an audition and don't get the job, shake it off and get fired up for the next one. Do your research, practice as much as possible and give it your all for each and every audition you go to. You've may have heard that Thomas Edison failed thousands of times before he ever created the electric light bulb. You must take the same determined approach if you're to succeed as a host. I can honestly say I have failed hundreds of times in my career, not only in hosting, but in many careers I've been a part of. And each time I do, I view it as one step closer to right job for me. Stay persistent, confident and positive as you go through this process. Doing so will put you at the front of the line and have you ready for the right opportunity when it presents itself.

As you begin to examine these seven attributes and how they relate to your personality, you may find that you have areas that need some improving, or you may find that you're perfectly suited to pursue this career because these seven attributes describe you to a "T." Either way, these qualities serve as a guide to where you are currently and what you need to improve to become a successful host. We all need a map to get started on a journey, and this book will serve as yours as you venture through the world of TV hosting.

Chapter 2

THE MIND GAME

"The top players in every field think differently when all the marbles are on the line. Great performers focus on what they are doing – and nothing else. They let it happen; let it go. They could care less about the results." – John Eliot

No doubt at some time in your life have you seen a television show that wasn't good. Maybe the storyline lacked punch, the premise was awful or maybe the host lacked a certain watchable quality. Many times when a host does poorly on a television show, it isn't necessarily because they lack talent; it tends to stem from the host being the wrong fit for the show format or premise. Other times it's a lack of good marketing, and then there is the rare occurrence when a show is simply directed toward the wrong audience.

Take Jay Leno, for instance, when he decided to give up *The Tonight Show* in 2009. The show originally aired at 10:30 p.m. NBC then decided to create *The Jay Leno Show,* which aired at 9 p.m. Just an hour and half difference, right? Wrong! The audience at 9 p.m. wasn't used to monologues and comedy. They were *Law & Order* watchers and had more of a taste for drama. Did the *Jay Leno Show's* poor ratings mean that Jay Leno was a bad host? Of course not! It's a textbook case of show concept that was placed in the wrong time slot for its ideal audience.

Ryan Seacrest, who is now considered the top-earning host on TV besides Oprah, launched a daily entertainment/variety/talk syndicated TV talk show in 2004 called *On Air with Ryan Seacrest*. However, even with Ryan's cult-like fan base, the show was cancelled due to low ratings nine months later. The reason I tell you this is because no matter how good a host you are, there is a good chance you will run into obstacles or setbacks along the way. The one hard truth about the hosting business is that it can be a tough road. Anytime you put yourself in front of a large audience and you voice an opinion or portray a certain personality, it's an inevitable truth that you won't please everyone out there. A reporter once asked comedian Bill Cosby about the secret to success. Bill replied, "I don't know what the secret of success is, but I know the secret to failure and that is to try and please everybody." I know I speak for many of us in the business when I say that some days, you just have to let go of what happened and keep moving forward with a positive attitude. You are you for a reason, and if a few people don't like the way you do something, that's THEIR problem and not yours. The fact that you have the courage to put yourself out there to be judged, good or bad, puts you among a small percentage of people. I, for one, applaud your courage, and I'm here to tell you that no matter what anyone tells you, you CAN do it! Be proud that you have confidence in yourself and your abilities, and let that be your foundation as you move forward.

Let me help you understand something. Your career is much like a competitive sporting event. There are plans, tactics and skill involved in coming out on top at the end of a game. How you plan your game in the hosting business will determine how many times you fail and how many times you put yourself in the position to succeed. I have talked to many hosts who say it's been nothing but an amazing time and they've hardly come across any negatives since they started! Others will tell you it has been a hellish climb to get to where they want to be, and they still struggle to this day trying to land a good host gig.

I have tasted both sides of the hosting experience. I had years when everything was smooth sailing and I didn't have a worry in the world about my career. Then there have been years where I was literally struggling to put food on the table as a freelance host. But it doesn't have to be that way for you. I went through some of these incredibly challenging times because I didn't have much of the information I am sharing with you in this book. If I would've had this knowledge five or 10 years ago, it would have likely launched my career into an entirely different stratosphere of success.

Probably the biggest and most important piece of advice I can share with you is that you must develop the right mindset when you decide to pursue the hosting business. There are literally thousands, if not millions, of people out there wanting to be the overnight success story that becomes the host of their own show. Just go to auditions for some of the major network shows and you'll see what I'm talking about. They're filling arenas just to audition! But no matter how big the crowds or how daunting the competition, the jobs will always go to those who work the hardest, are the most talented and who understand how the business works. You must be focused on perfecting your craft, knowing what types of projects will best suit your personality and making plans to succeed. Unless you are a high-ranking celebrity with millions of followers or you made front page national news in a big way, then, like the rest of us, you have to learn the game of becoming a host and how best to win it. There will be many opportunities to take different paths in your hosting career, and each decision you make will have a domino effect on where you go and what jobs you're in the running for. Over the past few years, I have interviewed many hosts and experts in the industry. As I compiled my information and began to compare my sources' recommendations, I saw three unique patterns that were key in their eventual success: simple mindsets that gave them a mental edge over the competition.

1. BELIEVE YOU CAN DO IT – We all have unique gifts and abilities that can be turned into successes and this must be your mental approach. If you believe you can't, failure will be a self-fulfilling prophecy. If you display a lack of self-belief when you're auditioning and talking to the camera, audiences and casting directors will pick up on it immediately and won't watch you or hire you. Successful hosts are not afraid to show the world who or what they are. One of the best examples of this in recent memory is daytime talk show host Ellen Degeneres. In 1997, she was the first lead in a sitcom to openly acknowledge her homosexuality on the air. Today, she continues to embrace who she is and what she stands for, and she isn't worried about how the world perceives her. Take the time to watch her and you'll see what I mean. She carries a confidence about herself that is undeniable.

2. THERE IS A JOB JUST FOR YOU - There are more than enough opportunities available for you to become highly successful. Many people believe there's "too much competition." This stops them from trying. The truth is, there are new opportunities being created every day and the next one may very well be perfect for you. But just because the opportunities are available doesn't mean you know about them. Many people miss the opportunities because they're not trying to find them. You must constantly be searching for the right gig for you, and you MUST BELIEVE that it is out there waiting for you.

3. CREATE YOUR OWN OPPORTUNITIES - Understand that sometimes you have to create your own opportunities instead of strictly paying attention to the casting calls and auditions. In my case, for several years now, I've recognized that there were no solid resources, outside of LA or NYC coaching programs, to give aspiring hosts advice and information on how to get into the business. I saw this as a

massive opportunity to add value where others didn't, and as a result I was able to write this book and offer it to you! Those who go out and create instead of following what everyone else is doing are always the ones leading the pack and getting the jobs. Successful people in any business, not just hosting, know this to be true. Understand that you are responsible for your results, even though there are many challenges outside of your control. It's your responsibility to create opportunities for yourself. When you take responsibility for results, it allows you to do a much better job of creating more opportunities to succeed. Take Wal-Mart founder Sam Walton's advice: "Swim upstream; go the other way. Ignore the conventional wisdom. If everybody else is doing it one way, there's a good chance you can find your niche by going exactly the opposite direction – but be prepared for a lot of folks to wave you down and tell you you're headed the wrong way."

Those three mindsets may be the most telling in the success of many hosts, but they are just the tip of the iceberg. Here's 10 more pieces of great advice not only from hosts themselves, but from coaches, casting directors and producers. They are all actions you can take to keep you on the right path to achieving success in your hosting career.

1. *Always be you!*
No matter what audition you go into, it's incredibly important that you be YOU. Don't try to change into what the casting director is looking for. If a particular job doesn't fit your personality, there will be another one out there that does. The last thing you want to do is land a job you had to fake it to get, and then end up "faking it" for months while recording episodes. You will be wasting not only your own time, but also the time of the entire crew.

2. DON'T play politics

If you try to manipulate people and situations to give yourself a leg up on the competition, you will scar your reputation in this business forever. If you bad mouth somebody or make a bad name for yourself in one circle, word spreads. This is a small business, and there are only a few degrees of separation between everyone in it. So build a reputation for integrity when developing professional relationships in this industry. Remember everything has its time, and when you do make a move, it will be because you're ready to make that move. You'll have done the work and prepared yourself, and you'll be able to perform on the level to which you aspire with the success you deserve.

3. Develop good relationships

As I mentioned before, this is a very small business. So, if you are good to somebody, that gets around … and vice versa. Network with anyone and everyone. You never know who may be able to help you out. Shake hands, pass out business cards and demo reels, and develop a Rolodex of EVERYONE you meet in the industry. It's likely that somewhere down the road, you will cross paths with them again.

4. Be ready when opportunity knocks

I once heard Oprah define the term "luck" as the merger that occurs when preparation meets opportunity. So, if the job of your life comes along and you haven't been practicing, you haven't been networking and you haven't been polishing your on-camera skills, there's likely someone else out there who has, and chances are they will get the job. You must believe at all times that your dream shot could come at any moment, and you MUST be prepared to perform when it comes.

5. Don't be outworked

I believe that success has two major ingredients. One is actual talent. True talent is a God-given quality that is undeniable.

Some people are simply born with the personality to be a host. If you have invested your time and money in this book, you must believe you have that talent. More importantly, the second ingredient – the one that actually towers above the talent – is good old-fashioned HARD WORK. No matter how much talent you have, unless you spend the time and do the work, you have zero chance of becoming anything great. The top people in any field often come to the realization they are truly not that special or different, they're just persistent. They have learned to never take NO for an answer. So I say to all of you, no matter what stage of your career you're at, start your dreams today! Work 10 times harder than the person who started 10 years earlier, and you still have every chance of beating them to the finish line. Besides, we should all measure our success on the inside. Do you want to host and be happy? Or do you want to host and make money? Each one of those sounds sweet, but it's even sweeter if you actually achieve both at the same time.

6. *Don't waste valuable time*

Understand that you need to take advantage of every second of every day! The fact is most of us don't spend as much time as we'd like actually hosting or speaking in front of a camera or audience. The idea that actual hosting jobs will eventually add up to give you the camera time you need to achieve greatness is not a wise way to look at it. If you only get to host a segment or show once a month, it will take you forever to be consistently comfortable on camera. You need to create a situation where you're practicing and performing all day every day. When you're at the market or grocery store speaking to someone, that one person is your audience. Make that your time to practice your interviewing and ad-lib skills. Make every one-on-one meeting you have add up to a great deal of performance time. The best time to perform and practice is in your daily life. Those moments add up fast and make you the best host you can be.

7. *Have confidence in yourself*

We covered this a bit in Chapter 1, but how others accept, believe in and perceive you depends on how you accept, believe in and perceive yourself. When I'm on camera, I'm excited but never nervous. Why should I be nervous? Nervousness and fear are for people who don't practice. When people ask me if I ever get nervous, my answer is always, "I only get nervous when I'm not prepared." You must accept yourself for who and what you are. You must be satisfied with what you know when you step in front of the camera. You must deliver your performance in a way that is truthful to you. You may not be a professional-athlete or brain surgeon, but you are a host who is really good at being YOU. If you can accept what you are and are not, and perform from a place of self-confidence, that is what the audience will perceive and connect with. It's not that you know everything, but that you feel great about your personality and abilities. With sufficient self-confidence, you could jump on camera with a lisp and an eye patch and still sell it. If you're OK with who you are and show the audience that you accept yourself, they will do the same. In fact, they will applaud your imperfections and the way you boldly display your freedom to be imperfect. What are you self-conscious about showing your audience? Find it and work to overcome your fear of it on camera.

8. *Set goals*

The fact that you're investing your time and money in this book tells me that you are serious about improving your skills and getting a job as a host! So, what's your plan? Do you have a particular show or program you want to be on? Do you have your sights set on a particular casting call? Are you unsure? You need to set goals, several different types of goals, and MAKE SURE you write these down. When you wake up every day and look at your goals, it reminds you that you need to be doing something each day to achieve them!

Start with short-term goals, and what I mean by this is, figure out what you want to accomplish over the next 30 days. Do you want to audition for a certain number of shows? Do you want to make a certain amount of contacts? Make sure that your goal is measurable. That way, you can gauge each and every day whether you're making the right amount of progress to achieve it.

Next, set your one-year goals. What do you want to look back on at the end of this year and say? That you landed a particular gig? That you're working full time at your craft? Or maybe that you reached a certain income level? Set goals that are meaningful for you.

Lastly, set a 10-year goal. Now before you do this, remember that a decade is a long time, so goals that might seem almost impossible right now can be attained over a 10-year period. Shoot for the stars here! If you want to host one of the major reality shows on the big networks, like *American Idol* or *Biggest Loser*, make that your goal. Then do everything you know to do, each and every day, to make sure you're ready for the opportunity when it presents itself!

9. *Have an optimistic attitude*

There has never been a better time to be a host. I don't care if you're just starting out or you're a veteran of this industry! The proliferation of reality television over the last decade has networks scrambling to get new programming on the air all the time, and you very well may be the exact personality type they're looking for! Remember, if you're prepared when the opportunity comes, lady luck will welcome you with open arms! And **don't give up if you really want this! There is no recipe for guaranteed success, and there's always some reason to be negative ... BUT DON'T BE! Just keep giving it your best!**

10. *Talk to yourself daily*

What many of us don't understand is that lasting motivation takes more than the occasional self-help book, coach or motivational speaker. While motivational talks are a great way to get in the right frame of mind, an hour or two of someone telling us that "we can do it!" simply doesn't cut it. The intentions are great. The talk is inspiring. The ideas are incredible. But when the coach or "external motivator" goes away – so does the motivation. Our poorly programmed subconscious mind takes over and we end up undercutting ourselves with self-doubt and self-criticism.

Yes, we want to believe in ourselves and our success, but entrenched negative thinking stops us cold with phrases like, "That will never happen" or "This is completely unrealistic" or "I'm wasting my time!" It's not about whether or not you are capable of succeeding; you ARE. But it comes down to combating the old, negative thoughts your mind has been feeding you for years!

Think of negative thinking like faulty software on a computer. No matter how hard you try to make it do what you want, the glitch in the internal software will always block you from doing so. That is, unless you change what's going on inside! It's time to update your internal software and upgrade your expectations.

So I'm going to give you a resource to help you.

If you can change your subconscious mind, get rid of those old negative thoughts and replace them with new, positive ones, you've programmed your internal software to subconsciously guide you toward what you want. This is the most fertile ground for growth and achievement that you will ever find.

Imagine having a "coach" that stayed with you season after season and every day in between. Imagine being able to rely on yourself to always automatically and unconsciously energize yourself, focus your attention and keep you moving in the right direction! INTERNAL motivation will be your closest ally, your strongest believer and your best friend.

I'm not talking about some sort of hypnosis or subliminal mumbo jumbo. This is a conscious personal decision you are making for yourself to help YOU get better on the inside. You are taking responsibility, and that means YOU are in control of the results.

What I am telling you is that when you learn to talk to yourself in the right way, when you apply the attributes of confidence, conviction and hard work, the inner strength you desire will begin to show up without your even trying. Now, before you go off thinking you need to get up every morning, look in the mirror and say "I'm good enough, I'm strong enough, and people like me!" continue reading.

For any self-improvement concept to work effectively, I've learned that it needs to be simple, easy to use, and when put into practice it MUST show results. If you go to the following link, www.timtialdo.com/resources you'll find a resource that I made specifically for you. It is filled with positive self-talk that will train your subconscious mind to get rid of the old, negative trash and replace it with new, positive thoughts. All you need to do is listen to it as often as possible. For the most effective results, listen to this once in the morning and once in the evening. Regardless of the time of day, two times each day should be VERY effective in changing your thought process. Remember, as motivational speaker Les Brown often says, faith comes by hearing and hearing and hearing!

Remember, your old self-talk is likely a negative habit, and in the first day or two, it will show its ugly head and tell you this stuff is a bunch of nonsense. But by knowing what to expect and by continuing to listen, you will begin to override those thoughts.

By replacing your earlier negative self-talk with new, positive commands, you're activating healthy, productive chemical and electrical control centers in your brain, which will automatically work for you instead of against you. When this happens, the new goals you set are more likely be accomplished and achieved

Exercise:

1. It's valuable to look at where you'll be in your career in the future so you can have a "map" for the journey of your career. Write

a vision for what you want your career to look like and where you want to be in 30 days, one year and 10 years. Write it in the present tense. "I wake up today in my new house, and I check my inbox to find several offers to host for network shows." OR "I will make $10,000 this month, having been the number one show on television for three seasons …"

2. Next, write down the key mindset or belief you'll need to get to each of your goals.

3. Download the MP3 from my website and begin listening to it at least once each day.

☐ Expert Tip: Put a notepad next to your bed and every morning and night; rewrite your vision and your mindset. Do this for the next 30 days. It'll take your results to the next level.

Chapter 3

---•---

PUT ME IN COACH

"A coach is someone who can give correction without causing resentment." – John Wooden

I read an interesting statistic in the Harvard Business Review that stated the top three reasons coaches are hired:

1. Develop potential or facilitate transition – 48%
2. Act as a sounding board – 26%
3. Address a derailing behavior – 12%

In the hosting business most of us fall under No. 1. We know we have it inside of us to do great things and be a real success, but we need someone to show us the way. No. 2 is for those who have been in the business for a while. They're professionals and they know their way around a camera, studio and crowd, but they are always looking to improve in any way they can. And then there's category No. 3. This is for those who never really learned the fundamentals of being on camera. Their delivery is equivalent to a teenager learning how to play basketball on the playground. They watched, learned and did what they thought was best with no coaching and no path to follow. While someone who goes out and does the work deserves admiration, a coach can take all that dedicated energy and focus it on the right tasks that would help them become a fantastic talent.

In most great success stories, you'll find a great coach or mentor behind the star. In sports, for example, Michael Jordan readily admits that much of the reason he is now a basketball legend is the principles he learned from his greatest coach, Dean Smith of the University of North Carolina. Upon his 2009 induction into the basketball Hall of Fame, Michael was asked who got him there. He answered, *"Dean Smith, in all honesty. The man that he made of me, along with my basketball talents that he elevated to another level and his knowledge of the game, giving me an opportunity to play, there is no way you would have got the chance to see Michael Jordan play without Dean Smith teaching me the game."*

Famed life coach and peak performance specialist Tony Robbins admits that much of his knowledge about the personal development industry came from his mentor and coach Jim Rohn. At one of his "Date with Destiny" events, Tony spoke about Jim right after his passing in 2010. *"He gave me a way to look at life; allowed me to ask not that life be easier, but to ask that I be better. He got me to realize that the secret to life was to work harder on myself than my job or anything else, because then I'd have something to give to people."*

American Idol host Ryan Seacrest learned many of his principles from his idol and mentor Merv Griffin. In an interview with Oprah Winfrey, Seacrest stated, *"He taught me a lot. He taught me how to leverage. He taught me how to take the success of being a personality and the access you have and build something to have forever; to build an asset. Because you never know how long this is going to last."*

The point I'm trying to make here is that no matter how talented you are, no matter how driven you are, having someone there to guide you down the path and keep you focused can mean the difference between mediocrity and living the life of your dreams. Experience and research shows that many aspiring hosts have the energy and drive to that could take them to the top, but a large majority have no idea how to do it. They try everything under the sun and often end up spinning their wheels because they just don't know where to turn for help. A good coach can be the answer, if you're willing to put forth the effort and time to learn from them.

I remember in 1995, when I sat down with a school counselor and started looking into colleges that offered anything that had to do with being a TV host, and found … nothing. There were courses for journalism, theatre, performance and storytelling but none that specifically focused on "hosting." Today there may be a few classes offered here and there as an "extra," but the very best way to truly learn to host is to work with people who are in the industry and in the know. Check out all the different types of courses and classes host coaches are now teaching:

- Hosting Boot Camps
- Showcases for Agents
- Brand Building Seminars
- Game Show Hosting
- Shopping Channel Workshops
- Improv Classes
- Teleprompter Reading Classes
- Backstage Interview Training
- Ear Prompter Training
- Training for Vloggers and Web Hosts
- Voice Coaching

If you want to be on-camera as a host, there's training for just about every genre in existence.

While you might spend upwards of $20,000 to $100,000 on your college education, today you can take some pretty dynamic and effective hosting courses for under $1,000. It's important that you take advantage of these courses, because in my experience, one hour with a host coach is worth 18 hours spent in school trying to learn what professors referred to as "performance."

Host Coaching

A great way to jump start your hosting career is simply to get into a hosting class, workshop or boot camp. Most of these range in price from a couple hundred bucks and up, but rarely have I seen any type of host coaching over $1,000. These courses are very effective because they focus solely on hosting, and the coaches keep class sizes small and intimate to allow for more one-on-one personal attention. This also means they fill up very quickly, so I advise that you constantly check coaches' websites and calendars below to see when the next courses are offered.

Instead of making you do hours of research, let me give you some guidance. These days, there are a handful of coaches who really stay in close contact with industry producers, casting directors, agents and current on-air hosts. Some of them are even casting directors and agents themselves. In my opinion, they are the gold standard when it comes to host coaches and I highly recommend their services:

Maureen Browne - http://initiativetalentgroup.com/
Marki Costello – http://www.becomeahost.com/
Robin Radin - http://www.robinradin.com/
Patricia Stark - http://www.patriciastark.com/

Each one of these coaches has her own style and methods. I encourage you to read up on each of them and watch any videos they have. This will give you a good idea of which one might best suit your personality and style.

Let me give you fair warning. There's a ton of "coaches" out there who like to say they do "on-camera" training, but let me give you some advice I learned the hard way. Much like learning the fundamentals of any sport, the first coach or coaches that you allow to work with you will develop the core talent and on-camera skills you'll always take with you. Make sure the methods of delivery and the presentation skills they're teaching you are for hosting in particular.

Being in the business for quite a while now, I can tell you that it's very easy to spot someone who hasn't learned the fundamentals of being a host. If you work with someone who really doesn't know what casting directors want to see or what audiences really crave from hosts, you're just digging a hole that you'll eventually have to climb back out of. Trust me; this is a frustrating experience that can take years to reverse. In my personal experience, I began in TV news and developed a "box" mentality that took me about two years to break out of. If you've ever watched a news program, you'll notice that anchors and reporters don't make many movements outside of their head and arms. News tends to be a serious atmosphere, and the lack of movement is simply the nature of that side of the business. But when you become a host, you'll find the more movements you make, the better. Watch any great host on a reality TV show and you'll see that they are always moving around, making big gestures and letting their body language do much of the talking. Coaches are great at helping you learn this!

Voice Training

Another VERY important aspect of a great host is how they use their voices. You'll notice that all great hosts make you feel like they're talking to their best friend. Much of that has to do with the way they use voice inflection, tone, melody and pace. A Stanford study shows that 93% of your ability to influence others is determined not by the actual words you say, but by how you sound and what your body does when you speak. In the hosting world, your personality is EVERYTHING so you can understand why voice training is incredibly important!

To learn how to use your voice correctly, you can take courses in person, over the phone and there are now even CD audio courses. Vocal coach Roger Love is considered the top voice coach in Hollywood. Roger has worked with a slew of celebrity voices from Reese Witherspoon, Tyra Banks and Tony Robbins, to the cast of Glee. He recently created a CD audio course you can order online that is incredibly helpful and one I use daily while driving in my car. It's called "The Perfect Voice" and you can find it at www.theperfectvoice.com. It costs around $100. His CD course will teach you how to use your voice and how to fix any problems you might already have. Roger is also available for one-on-one coaching.

If you're looking to do voice training in a one-on-one setting, one of the other great coaches out there is a man by the name of Marc Cashman. I had the great pleasure of doing some one-on-one training over the phone with Marc and got great results from our one-hour sessions. He conducts classes in his California studio or you can schedule phone sessions like I did. Either way, Marc is a veteran of the voice acting profession and has an extensive background in educating others on how to effectively use their voices. Check out Marc's website www.cashmancommercials.com

Coach Yourself to Begin

Even before you invest your money in a coach, you can start coaching yourself right now by doing simple things:

- Use your phone or flip cam and start recording your own segments.
- Read out loud every day from a book or magazine to get your teleprompter skills up to par.
- Listen to what the popular hosts out there say and do. Watch how they address the camera. You'll see that most good hosts aren't afraid to do something different and be themselves.
- Practice interviewing friends and colleagues, and don't be afraid to add some of your own personal flavor to make it fun and engaging!
- Start testing your quick-witted responses with friends during casual conversation and see what kind of reaction

you get. Are they laughing? Confused? Smiling? This will help you gauge how your audience will respond.

- Let other people watch and listen to what you record. Get their feedback. Many times we tend to look at ourselves and only see what's working; we overlook what might not be working. Most of the people who will be watching you as a host are not in the business and they'll give you honest feedback. You need to get used to hearing this!

- Lastly, as I mentioned this earlier, start doing you own webisodes! Get a YouTube Channel and a Facebook fan page, and post to them as often as possible! This is a great way to prepare you for the real thing when the right opportunity comes along. It will also show casting directors that you're diligent and working hard, and that's always a plus!

Find A Mentor

In addition to having a coach, it's also a great idea to have a mentor in your life. A mentor is typically someone who befriends you because they love to help others reach success and they see a "certain something" in you that they can develop. A good mentor will also have years of experience in the area in which you want to be successful. You read at the beginning of this chapter how people like Michael Jordan, Tony Robbins and Ryan Seacrest all had great mentors who also served as coaches.

In my life, I have had the great fortune of having several high-profile mentors in multiple areas of expertise. Some were in sports, others in marketing and finance, and others in TV; however, my first mentor was Nancy O' Dell, who is now the co-host of *Entertainment Tonight*. At the time (2000), I was part of the research department at *Access Hollywood*, which is on the NBC Studios lot. Since our offices and studios were in separate buildings, I would frequently be asked to run over to the studio to help out. Every time I did, I always took an extra couple of minutes to sit in the green room with Nancy and pick her brain about the TV business. She used to tell me how she remembered being a one-man-band news reporter in South Carolina and having to measure her on-camera height with the lighting equipment before she rolled on a take. A couple of years later, when she was the host of *Nashville Star*, she invited me down to Tennessee to be backstage for a taping of the show. Nancy always had great charm and was very willing to give me any advice I was searching for. At one point, to help me out, she introduced me to her agent at the time, Ken Linder, who is legendary in the TV agent biz. When you have someone like Nancy in your life, someone who is willing to go out of her way to help you, be sure to take advantage of the opportunity and be gracious to that person in return. After all, they are investing their time and experience in your success.

The great thing about having a mentor is they can save you years of frustration by giving you simple advice or suggesting steps you would have never thought of on your own. If you don't currently have mentors in your life, don't panic. The first person you reach out to may not become a lifelong mentor, but keep reaching out to people you respect and admire. I remember when I was a news anchor in Clarksburg, WV. While watching the Pittsburgh, PA, morning news and preparing for my own show, I happen to recognize one of the anchors. She was a woman I used to watch in my hometown of St. Louis, MO. Her name was Wendy Bell, and she was a former feature reporter for a show called *Show Me St. Louis*. I loved watching her because her personality was infectious, her storytelling was hilarious and other people loved watching her. Since we were both now in the business and she was nearby, I simply went to the Pittsburgh TV station website, found her contact info and sent her a very complimentary and honest email that explained how I would love to get some mentoring from her. She was flattered, and for the next year, once a month, I visited her morning show in Pittsburgh. On each visit she spent several hours with me: critiquing my stories, helping better my presentation and motivating me to go after everything I wanted.

Having both a mentor and coach is without a doubt one of the best things you could ever do to raise your hosting career to a new level of excellence. Start researching, start evaluating and take that step! If you're low on funds, do the home exercises first and save up for one of the workshops or boot camps. That may mean you need to stay in a few nights instead of going out to help pay for it, but I promise you, it's one of the best investments you'll ever make! Remember, this is your life and your career.

Surround Yourself with Succcess

The above steps are important to your development as a host and on-camera personality, but there's something even more important to your personal development. You need to set the stage for success in your career and life by surrounding yourself with the right people!

A unique trait of human social development is that we tend to become like the people we surround ourselves with. Research has shown that if you take the five people closest to you and average them (their personalities, attitudes and values) you get YOURSELF.

Most people who know me well know that I'm very particular about who I allow into my inner circle. If you're going to turn into the people you surround yourself with, then success needs to be part of their makeup. Who are you surrounding yourself with and why? When you hang out with people on a regular basis, whether you know it or not, they are influencing your development. I challenge you to take an inventory of the people that you allow to affect your daily life and see if they're giving you the best chance of succeeding.

I'm not trying to get you to break up relationships or defriend anyone in your life; all I'm trying to say is that you need to be critical of the people and conditions you allow into your life, so that success naturally emerges from your interactions with them.

As an example, one of my coaching clients and very good friends is Ms. Figure Olympia, Nicole Wilkins. Nicole is the No. 1 figure competitor in the world and can often be seen gracing the covers of the top fitness magazines. When we're together, I see why she is so successful. She is very detailed, punctual and driven. She is constantly trying to improve not only her physique, but also her professional skills, marketing skills and attitude in general. Her work ethic is infectious, and I find that when we are around each other, there is a definite feeling of success in the room. It's great to have people like that around you. They push you, inspire you and make you want to be better at whatever it is you're doing.

Your success comes from a myriad of things. When you're young, you identify your talent; in school, you work on developing that talent; in your career, you look for opportunities to use that talent; and eventually you find the connections that match your talent with someone that can use it. By setting the conditions for success, you're allowing it to happen on its own.

There are two crucial questions you need to be asking yourself right now:

1. Who do I need to become so I can take advantage of the opportunities?
2. What people do I need to surround myself with so I become who I want to become?"

If you have successful friends already, fantastic! You're literally in good company and setting yourself up for major growth in your life and career. If you don't have such friends, this is easily one of the toughest concepts to accept on the road to success: Some of the people you like and who like you … are actually holding you back, and you need to let go of some of them to reach your goals.

I know this sounds difficult, but let me explain. Don't start by kicking people out of your life. Rather, start finding successful people to add to your circle as often as possible. The people you love are still in your life, but as you add more successful people to your circle and spend more time learning from and associating with them, negativity – and negative people – will gradually be marginalized.

If you're not having the success you want in your life, it's almost certain that you don't have "successful" people in your circle. There is no better time to start than right now.

Exercise:

1. Make a list of the people you'd like to add to your inner circle. You may know them or not. Look for people who have the success you'd like to create. Identify three people you're going to befriend over the next three months. Reach out, ask if they'll have lunch with you, and ask them a few questions.

2. Create a list of three people you'd like to get as mentors. Your goal is to get one of them as your mentor. When they give you advice, do what they say and report back to them on the results. That can really solidify the mentoring relationship.

Chapter 4

GET SPECIFIC

"The indispensible first step to getting the things you want out of life is this: decide what you want." – Ben Stein

egendary business guru and influential author Peter Drucker once used a very powerful phrase that stuck with me: "Strengthen your strength." This means you must not focus excessively on your weaknesses, and don't ignore the fact that your natural talents will shape the opportunities that have the most potential for you.

As a host, expertise is your strength. I define expertise as knowledge + experience. The more you develop your knowledge and experience, the more valuable you become. No matter what genre of hosting you decide to pursue, work on improving things like your vocabulary, your ability to persuade, using metaphor and story, and speaking in front of an audience. The better you are at doing all these things, the better you will be on-camera, period.

As I talked about in Chapter 2, picking a show or program to audition for without first asking yourself if you're right for it is a recipe for disaster in the hosting industry. To develop our God-given talents into strengths, we must do what doesn't always come to us naturally – and that's to narrow our focus and our expertise. If you have really deep expertise in a particular area, let's say interviewing others, and that's part of your natural talent or gifts, then that's likely where you'll succeed! But this "narrowing" of your focus and skills can be uncomfortable for many.

Let's say you've decided that being a game show host is where your greatest talents lie. If so, then you don't want to spend most of your time learning about all the different areas of hosting like reality shows, shopping channels or talk show hosting. Instead, spend about 80 percent of your time focusing on that segment of hosting that is most suited to your natural talents and your personal and professional growth.

If you get into hosting and you try to be a talk show host, and you then you experiment with being a game show host, and you see that you're definitely better at the game show stuff… it would make perfect sense for you to narrow your focus on game show hosting. There's nothing wrong with being interested in something that's not perfectly suited for what you thought was your skill set. If something else comes along and you find it comes naturally to you, that's a great thing! Be smart and follow it.

For me, becoming an emcee for charities and professional sports teams was a real eye-opening way to improve my skills on camera. I found that when I was live in front of these large audiences ranging from 500 to 50,000 people, it made my awareness of everything around me that much stronger. Then when I went back into the studio, I found the teleprompter easier to read, interviews were less nerve-racking and my general performance on camera improved greatly.

That being said, I want to give you some help in narrowing down what your focus in hosting should be. It's likely that many of you reading this already know exactly what you want to do, but knowing all your options before you get started is essential. I find that many people don't know all the opportunities out there that might match their talents, so let me break down the most popular and well-known styles of hosting that are out there today.

Spokesmodel/Spokesperson

A spokesmodel or spokesperson is someone whose appearance and personality contributes to a company's brand. Good examples of hosts who have gone on to become spokespersons include Mike Rowe (Ford, Lee) Ty Pennington (Sears, Lumber Liquidators), Jillian Michaels (Go Daddy) etc. As we will cover in upcoming chapters, understanding your brand is essential to your foundation as a host. Just like a company, once you know what the brand is, you begin to target a certain audience. What many hosts are surprised to find later in their careers is that the same audience they cater to happens to be the same audience a large company or corporation caters to. For those companies, this makes many hosts a perfect spokesperson for their brand because they already have an established relationship with the target audience.

Infomercial Host

Infomercial hosts appear on long-form television commercials, which typically range from 15 to 30 minutes, and short-form infomercials, which are typically 30 seconds to 2 minutes long.

Infomercials were originally created as a form of television advertising; however "infomercials" can refer to any video presentation that offers a significant amount of information to promote a point of view. They're also known as paid programming.

As an infomercial host, you're basically a pitchman/woman selling whatever product or service a company pays you to present. The quality of infomercials tends to range from the very poor ones that air in the overnight hours, to some of the more well-produced ones endorsed by a celebrity infomercial host. Many hosts use infomercials as an extra source of income in addition to their main job, provided their contract allows it.

Some of the best-known infomercial hosts are the recently deceased Billy Mayes, Anthony Sullivan, former *Entertainment*

Tonight Host Leeza Gibbons, Tony Robbins, Tony Horton of P90X fame, and more recently, magazine show hosts like Mark Steines and Dana Devon have entered into this genre.

Home Shopping Host

A home shopping host partners with guests on network television shopping channels, such as HSN, QVC, and ShopNBC. The host's job is to introduce new presenters and guests to the television audience and help these guests explain the values and features of the products being showcased. Many of the guests who accompany the host on-air often aren't very TV-savvy or experienced, so a home shopping host must help guests better define the details and value of the items being showcased.

As a host in this role, you'll typically stay on the air for anywhere from one to five hours at a time, welcoming several new guests and demonstrating many new products. Since products and guests are often only given 10 or 15 minutes to sell in the world of home shopping, it's not uncommon for a host to be required to introduce 20 or more different products and inventions during their shift. Shopping networks are broadcast live, 24-hours a day, so mistakes and errors cannot be edited out. In this line of work, being quick-witted, personable and likeable is essential, as well as being able to make quick transitions from one product to another.

Networks also like to routinely debut new inventions and products, requiring the host to quickly explain to the audience why the item is worth purchasing. Because of the large number of guests and products, hosts often don't have the time to study products beforehand. An effective host should possess good verbal skills to mask this lack of direct product knowledge. Probably the best-known Home Shopping Host on TV today is former Miss Tennessee Lisa Robertson of QVC. She's been on the air since 1995.

Other notable shopping hosts are Kim Parrish, John Cremeans, Lisa Mason and Jennifer Crawford.

Reality TV Host

Probably the best-known types of hosts today are reality television hosts. This category of television programming is very broad, but popular. Reality hosts present unscripted dramatic or humorous situations, document actual events, and almost all reality shows feature ordinary people instead of professional actors, sometimes in a contest or other situation where a prize is awarded. The genre, as discussed in the introduction of the book, exploded as a phenomenon around 1999–2000 with the success of such television series as *The Bachelor* hosted by Chris Harrison, *The Amazing Race* hosted by Phil Keoghan and *Survivor* hosted by Jeff Probst. Since then, reality TV has expanded exponentially and covers a wide range of television programming formats, from game shows or quiz shows to voyeurism-focused productions such as *Big Brother* and *The Real World*.

While there is no set format for a Reality TV host, reality television tends to portray an influenced form of reality, at times utilizing sensationalism to attract audience viewers and increase advertising revenue profits. Product placement has become more prominent as the genre grows, as demonstrated on shows like *Extreme Makeover, Home Edition* and *The Biggest Loser*. Participants can be placed in exotic locations (*Survivor*) or abnormal situations (*The Bachelor*), and are often persuaded to act in specific scripted ways by off-screen "story editors" or "segment producers." Other forms of reality shows are those like *Top Chef, Mythbusters* and *What Not to Wear*. Each show establishes its own specific format and style and the hosts are crucial to making that format a success. *American Idol's* Ryan Seacrest is the most successful reality show host to date, signing a $45 million deal in 2009 and a new one on 2012, putting him in the payday ranks of professional athletes and Hollywood actors and actresses.

Internet and Web TV Host

This genre of TV has just recently started to gain mass popularity with shows like *Yahoo's Daytime in No Time* hosted by Nikki Boyer and *Prime Time in No Time* hosted by Frank Nicotero and even *Yahoo's Sports Minute*. With faster downloads and ease of accessibility through phones and tablets, you will see this genre grow exponentially over the next few years, and more and more hosting jobs will be popping up everywhere. If you want to get ahead of the curve, this is the genre you can do it in!

Vlog Host

Video blogging, also called vlogging is basically blogging with video. It's a form of Web TV in which a host can combine embedded videos or a video link with supporting text, photos and other information. You can record a vlog in one take or you can edit a series of takes into multiple parts. This has become one of the top categories on YouTube. Vlogging also allows hosts to take advantage of web syndication. This means you can distribute your videos over the Internet using either an RSS feed or playback on mobile devices and personal computers.

I highly recommend this genre for those of you starting out in your hosting careers. This is one of the best ways to get comfortable doing the day to day on camera stuff and increasing your confidence and developing a following. If you go on YouTube, you'll see that there are thousands, maybe even millions of people vlogging these days. But if you pay attention to the information I am providing you in this book, you will be able to put yourself at the front of the pack, establishing a strong vlogging presence in your own sphere of influence.

For example, 37-year-old Michael Buckley became an Internet celebrity when he created a vlog called *What the Buck?* in which he covers popular culture events and celebrities. He has one of YouTube's most popular channels with several million viewers each month. Michael started his vlog as a small weekly segment that gave him the freedom to rant on his own. His cousin then posted these rants on YouTube and it took off from there. He built a following and started his own YouTube channel in 2006, centering his focus on celebrities and pop culture, complete with satire and parodies. In 2008, he was making so much money on YouTube that he was able to quit his job for Live Nation. In April of 2008, Buckley started broadcasting live Internet TV shows on BlogTV. Those shows were viewed by over 200,000 people. In August 2010, he was a red carpet host for the 2010 Teen Choice Awards where he got the chance to interview TV, web and film stars.

Lifecasting Host

Lifecasting is when you broadcast daily events in your life through digital media channels like YouTube and Facebook. There are many different ways to do this, but the most successful "lifecasters" simply use camera and lighting equipment. Lifecasters can generate millions of viewers and companies wanting them to market their products. For years, major TV networks always held the power when it came to generating large audiences through TV viewership. YouTube has changed the game by giving individuals the ability to generate their own content that can be seen anywhere in the world. While "TV host" has been the longstanding term, now "lifecasters" are evolving what a host is and can become.

Easily the most recognizable and successful lifecaster is Justine Ezarik, better known as "iJustine." She has millions of followers on her channel, ijustine.tv. She's produced hundreds of videos which garner upwards of 30 million views each. She generated so much buzz about herself that when she created a video about wanting to order a cheeseburger, it generated 600,000 YouTube views in a week!

She also gained nationwide international media attention when she posted a video called the "300-page iPhone bill," which followed the first month of service after the introduction of the iPhone in 2007. She created so much bad publicity for AT&T that the corporate giant announced that detailed billing would become optional for iPhone users. Who said you need a TV network to make an impact? Her popularity also generated television guest appearances on *Law & Order: Special Victims Unit*, *Criminal Minds* and *The Bold & The Beautiful*.

She has been hired by MTV and Dick Clark Productions to host online pre-shows for awards broadcasts. Carl's Jr. has hired a team of YouTube stars, including Ezarik, to produce made-for-web ads for its new Portobello Mushroom Six-Dollar Burger on the Carl's Jr. menu. In December 2009, *USA Today* reported that Ezarik earned about $75,000 annually from YouTube. So for those of you who think money can't be made in hosting without being on TV, there's the evidence that yes you can!

Local Lifestyle Host

Normally produced by local network affiliate news stations, local lifestyle shows are a cross between news and entertainment. The host is able to dress more causally than a news anchor and tends to have more fun, fluffy material to talk about. Duties of a lifestyle show host tend to include on-set interviews, teleprompter reading, ad-lib segments on pop culture, feature reporting, and hosting live on location. These types of shows can be great stepping stones for future network hosts. Mike Rowe was the host of *Eye on the Bay* in San Francisco; Matt Lauer was the host of *PM Magazine* before heading to ESPN and later New York where he now anchors *The Today Show*.

I also was a local lifestyle host for two years and can attest that this style of hosting can be one of the best ways to prepare you for the next level. You're in front of large audiences and you tend to cover fun events that allow you to unleash your personality. Lifestyle shows also allow you to get out to of the studio atmosphere and away from the teleprompter, which helps you improve your ad-libbing skills. If you live in or near a city that has a show like this, start networking, preparing your materials and, when the opportunity comes along, apply and use the tactics I give you in this book to take advantage of it!

Professional Sporting Event Emcee or Host

If you've been to any professional sporting event, you've likely seen one of these hosts. Either in between innings or during a timeout or commercial break, they pop up on the big screen, usually doing some outrageous game with a fan or conducting trivia contests of some kind.

While these types of jobs are not very lucrative, they are a blast and they put you live in front of a ton of people. To do this job, you need to be funny, extremely outgoing and not be afraid of really big live audiences.

I and many other hosts that I know have had the great privilege of working for professional football, baseball and basketball teams as emcees and hosts. While we knew it wouldn't be our lifelong career, it is incredibly fun and can definitely lead to bigger and better jobs in the industry.

To find jobs like these and be considered for them, you must network and send in your materials to the right person. If you go on any professional sports team's website, most of them list the different departments you can contact. You should be looking for the "head of production." Send this person an email stating your desire to work for them and why you would be the best person for the job. At the very least, you'll likely get a response from them, if only because you were enough of a professional to approach the right person in the first place.

Game Show Host

This may historically be the most recognized type of host on TV. A game show host typically works on shows that range from a half hour to an hour long and involve some sort of prize(s). These are typically money, romance or a vacation of some kind. This format is one of the most successful in television history. Shows like *Wheel of Fortune* and *Jeopardy* have been on the air nearly 30 years and continue to be some of the highest rated syndicated shows on television. Game shows tend to be self-contained to one victorious outcome per episode, unlike reality competitions which span through weeks of episodes (i.e. *American Idol, Survivor*, etc.). So, that makes each episode an entirely new adventure for the hosts, contestants and the audience.

Some of the top game show hosts on TV are Alex Trebek (*Jeopardy*), Pat Sajack (*Wheel of Fortune*), Todd Newton (*Family Game Night*), Wayne Brady (*Let's Make a Deal*), Meredith Vieira (*Who Wants to Be a Millionaire*) and Drew Carey (*Price is Right*).

Talk Show Host

Talk shows are often identified by the host's name in the title, an indication of the importance of the host in the history of the television talk show.

Many talk show hosts come from a journalism background. Phil Donahue, Oprah Winfrey, Geraldo Rivera and Anderson Cooper all mix news, entertainment and public affairs together.

Entertainment talk shows are popular but have a limited number of formats. By far the most prevalent is the informal celebrity guest/ host talk show, which takes on different characteristics depending upon what part of the day it's shown. There are also whole ranges of shows that are not conventionally known as "talk shows" but feature "fresh" talk and are built primarily around that talk. These shows center on social encounters or events adapted to television:

a religious service (*The 700 Club*), a practical joke *(Punked)*, marriages (*The Marriage Ref*), legal cases (*Judge Judy*), or a social event (*New Years Rockin Eve).* The line between "television talk" and what formally constitutes a talk show is often not easy to draw, and it shifts over time as new forms of television talk emerge.

A good example of the importance of the host in shaping the form a talk show takes would be *The Tonight Show,* which changed significantly with each successive host. Steve Allen, Ernie Kovacs, Jack Paar, Johnny Carson and Jay Leno each took *The Tonight Show* in a significant new direction. Each of these hosts imprinted the show with distinctive personalities and management styles. Throughout the 1960s, 1970s and 1980s, Johnny Carson's monologue on the *Tonight* show was considered a litmus test of public opinion, a form of commentary on the news. Jay Leno's and David Letterman's comic commentary continues that tradition today.

The name Oprah likely comes to mind when you hear "talk show host" as she is easily the most powerful host in any genre. Oprah started in local media in the mid 1970s and was both the youngest news anchor and the first black female news anchor at Nashville's WLAC-TV. She moved to Baltimore's WJZ-TV in 1976 to co-anchor the 6 o'clock news. She was then recruited to co-host WJZ's local talk show *People Are Talking*, which premiered in 1978.

In 1983, Winfrey moved to Chicago to host WLS-TV's low-rated half-hour morning talk show, *AM Chicago.* The first episode aired in January of 1984. Within months, the show went from last to first place in Chicago's ratings, overtaking *Donahue* as the highest rated talk show in Chicago. She then signed a syndication deal with *King World.* The program was renamed *The Oprah Winfrey Show,* expanded to a full hour, and broadcast nationally beginning in September of 1986. Winfrey's syndicated show brought in double Donahue's national audience, displacing Donahue as the No. 1 daytime talk show in America. Her talk show *Oprah* became the highest rated program of its kind in history and made Oprah a billionaire. She has since ended *Oprah* and started OWN, the Oprah Winfrey Network, where she continues to host a variety of programs.

Magazine Show Host

Tabloid entertainment TV or entertainment newsmagazine shows are typically composed of breaking news stories, exclusive set visits, first looks at upcoming film and television projects, and one-on-one interviews with Hollywood talents and celebrities.

Popular magazine shows like *Entertainment Tonight, Access Hollywood, Extra* and *E! News Now* air as either half-hour or one-hour entertainment news shows. These types of shows also tend to have special correspondents who report on particular features for the show.

I had the great pleasure to work in the research department at *Access Hollywood* at the beginning of my career. We were located in a trailer on the lot of NBC studios and had a working crew of about 100 people total to put on a daily 30-minute program. Coming out of college, it was amazing to me the level of production and manpower it took to put on one of these shows. Our hosts at the time, Nancy O' Dell and Pat O' Brien, taught me a ton of great information and also were great role models to watch on a daily basis. Pat was a great writer and Nancy was super smooth with delivery and red-carpet interviews.

Overall I can tell you that if you want to be one of these types of hosts, there's no particular pre-requisite, although a previous stint in news or sports will greatly help you. Mario Lopez had neither of those and today is a great host for *Extra*. But unless you are a bona fide Hollywood celebrity, I highly recommend some sort of journalism job beforehand. That experience will help you with writing, researching, investigating and establishing a general sense of ease in the studio and in the field.

While there continue to be new hosting genres popping up all the time, the ones I've listed above are the most popular and have the most jobs available. As with anything, I always recommend you do your research and learn as much as you can about the particular genre you are targeting.

Exercise:

1. Write out a list of the types of hosts that you think you might be good at. Under each write which strengths you have that would make you a good host for that particular type of program. Once you see it on paper, this will help you learn which genre you should be focused on learning.

Chapter 5

---•✦•---

YOUR CALLING CARDS

"If you have a strong foundation, then you can build or rebuild anything on it. But if you've got a weak foundation, you can't build anything" – Jack Scalia

I'm a big fan of watching complicated projects come together and become successful. I was particularly fascinated in 2010 with the Burj Khalifa in Dubai, which at the time was being constructed as the world's tallest building. It is a staggering 2,717 feet tall – more than half a mile high – and easily overshadows the previous tallest building, located in Taiwan, which was 1,671 feet tall. To put that in perspective, it stands double the height of the renowned Empire State Building.

While most of our attention is focused on its height, perhaps more important is what lies beneath the building. Buried 164 feet beneath the Burj Khalifa lies over 120,000 tons of concrete to support this massive structure. Without a solid foundation, the world's tallest building would become the world's largest pile of rubble.

The same principle applies to a great hosting career. What people see and what we marvel about are the great heights to which some people seem to soar. Think about the people you admire right now and how you've likely followed their path and studied how they became a success. A heralded career is built on foundational principles like dependability and hard work.

Jesus said, "Everyone who hears these words of mine and puts them into practice is like a wise man who built his house on the rock. The rain came down, the streams rose, and the winds blew and beat against that house; yet it did not fall, because it had its foundation on the rock" (Matthew 7:24-25).

Your foundation matters. We cannot start wrong and expect to finish right. If your plan is to reach high in your hosting career, you must first start with a solid foundation. I have to honestly admit that, while I thought I had a great foundation when I got into hosting, unfortunately, I didn't; it cost me years of trying to "figure it out" as a result. When I first transferred over from news into hosting, I thought I knew exactly what I was supposed to do when it came to submitting my materials to casting directors. Boy, was I wrong! My resume was incorrectly formatted, my demo reel was WAY too long, and I didn't even have a solid headshot. Whether you are now in the business or are thinking about getting into it, you need to know that there are four branding materials that are "foundational columns" in the hosting world. They are your:

- Demo Reel
- Resume (One Sheet)
- Bio
- Headshots

These are your calling cards in the business, and agents and casting directors are very particular about what they like to see in them. I'm going to walk you through how to correctly develop each one of these to give yourself the best opportunity to become a network TV host!

Demo Reel

Let's first start with the most important calling card in the industry, and that's your demo reel. A demo reel in the host world is an absolute MUST. If you don't have a reel, as one casting director bluntly put it, "You're not a host!" But the good news is they're not that difficult or expensive to create. If you already have a reel this section will be a good review to make sure yours is edited correctly and has all the right material on it.

To create a host reel you need to do one of two things:

1) Hire a professional to edit your reel for you, OR
2) Find your own camera, an editor and use your own ingenuity

I personally love to go the professional route for several reasons. First, an unbiased evaluation of your material always helps because it forces you to hear what you'd likely hear from a casting director and audience anyway. If you do decide to take the professional route, one of the most important things you need to do is to get organized! When you hire a professional, you're not merely giving them a bunch of DVDs and video files and saying, "Good luck!" You and the video professional work as a team, and your job on that team is to provide your current materials to them in an organized fashion. If you have 10 or 20 DVDs with a bunch of different material on them, you should go through them first. If possible, log these and provide time codes for all the material on each DVD that you think might be good reel material. If you don't have the time to log all of them, at the very least make some notes pointing out the specific things on those DVDs that are good.

Before you get into producing and editing your reel, let's address exactly what a HOST reel is. There are different types of reels – from news to industrials to acting – and each requires something specific. It's not just a music video! A demo reel is all about you … this is your time, and it's not about who you interviewed or what event you were at. Brian Rose of Brose Productions is one of the top host reel editors in the business, and he provided a great explanation:

"When being considered for a job, there is a small window of time to impress and capture your audience while also convincing them that YOU are the one for the job. If produced correctly, a demo reel can be both brief, yet powerful, and convey all of the talent's strong points as well as highlight their distinctiveness and unsurpassed qualities. I look at each demo reel as a unique opportunity to visually express every one of my client's talents."

For a host reel, you first must know who you are and how you want people to perceive you as a host. Some good questions to ask yourself are:

What do you want to accomplish?
What's your niche?
What you are good at?
Are you funny?
Are you excitable?
Are you insane?
What makes you stand out from others?
Why should I watch you?

Your personality, your opinion and your point-of-view equal your "brand" to the world watching. Nobody wants to watch a dull and boring personality. People want to buy brands they enjoy, and so do the networks. If you think about it, there are a million channels these days and so many opportunities for hosting gigs. They want to hire a person or a brand that is going to stand out and create some talk about themselves! Why do you think Mike Rowe has endorsements from the Ford Motor Company and Lee Jeans? Why do you think Rachel Ray has tons of endorsements with food related companies? Because people are talking about them ALL THE TIME! What's your brand? Keep that question at the forefront of your mind.

What do you want the world to see you as?

The answer to this question will define your pathway. To give you a visual blueprint for what a good demo reel looks like, I've provided some great examples in each of the hosting genres on my website at www.timtialdo.com/resources.

How long does it need to be?

This is usually the first thing most people ask when it comes to developing a host reel. It's a great question, because while a news reel might be anywhere from 10 to 15 minutes, a host reel needs to be only 3 minutes in length, give or take 30 seconds. I interviewed well-known casting director and host coach Maureen Browne about what she likes to see on a reel, and this was her answer:

"I really want to see good stand-ups. If I'm looking in 30 seconds, I need to see that you know how to interview someone, that you have a really strong stand up and that you can really master reading copy. Interviewing someone, it doesn't have to be a celebrity, but I want to know that you are present and listening to them instead of thinking about what the next question is that you need to be asking them, because that is HUGE! Those are the two most important things I want to see in 30 seconds and, of course, your personality."

One of my favorite reels is of former QVC Shopping Host Kim Parrish. It's under 3 minutes, it's fast-paced, tells a great story and showcases exactly who Kim is and what she's about. You can check it out on my website at www.timtialdo.com/resources. Remember, the host demo reel is all about showing off your personality, your style, your look and your swagger. In those 3 minutes, you want to make sure that no one segment is too long, so each clip should go for no more than 10 seconds.

Now some of you are saying, "Well that's all good and fine, but I've got this great interview I did with so and so and the clip is 30 seconds." OK, here's how you handle that: You can do more than 10 seconds of an interview, but cut it up where you see bits and pieces throughout the 3 minutes rather than the whole interview clip straight. That way, if there's some good interaction, personality and humor, you can sprinkle that across the reel to keep it fun and engaging.

What Stands Out on a Hosting Reel?

Charisma – Remember in the first chapter when we said that charisma can't be taught? When an agent, casting director or production company watches a reel, it doesn't take long for them to spot the kind of charisma they're looking for. Most would tell you that within 30 seconds they have either spotted the talent they're looking for or not. So when you're producing your reel, make sure that that you put some of your best stuff up front to really grab their attention. Stuff that has energy! Go back and read exactly what Maureen Browne said in her interview. The reel should grab the viewer right off the bat. Otherwise, after those 30 seconds, they're going to throw it in the pile with all the others.

A sense of humor – Making people laugh is a quality that will NEVER go out of style. There's a reason that shows like *America's Funniest Home Videos* and the news blooper shows have been on so long. People love to laugh, and if you have the ability to make them do so, you're going to be a great host! So, any time you do something that you think is funny, showcase it, but pick your best stuff. And if you want to know it's truly funny (not just by your standards), let other people watch it and get their reactions. Sometimes we think what we did is funny when nobody else thinks that. Do those litmus tests with other people before you decide to include something in your reel.

Authenticity. You need to be a BIG personality without coming across as phony or unnatural. If it looks forced, you probably won't get the job. Make sure the content you're putting on the reel is authentic! Remember, the key here is just to be who you are and be truly comfortable in your own skin. Many of you watch great hosts out there like Tom Bergeron or Ty Pennington or Ellen Degeneres. What makes them great is that they don't follow the typical standard of what a host is supposed to be, they set their own standard because they're truly themselves; they're unique and their personalities literally carry the shows they are hosting. That's what agents and casting directors are looking for.

So, to review, the three things that stand out on a reel are:

- Charisma
- A sense of humor
- Authenticity.

Now let's get into overall expectations in terms of your content and variety of clips. As a general rule, the reel has to showcase you as a person and your personality. The reel needs to show your diversity and range, so consider having an interview clip, a clip where you're ad-libbing straight to the camera, maybe something where you're in the field, and another that's a teleprompter read. It's all about showing off your different "looks," i.e. how you look delivering various types of content. For instance, when you're interviewing someone in the field, that's a look. Reading from a teleprompter is a look. Be versatile. Give them clips that display your background and different types of material, and mix it up to show all of your qualities and attributes. If you're crazy goofy, then let your reel show that! If you're dry-humored or great at quick-witted humor in interviews, make sure the reel reflects that. Show all sides of your personality… comedic, serious, zany, insightful, etc.

The next area to cover that's particularly relevant to current reality show trends is specialization. What if you're an expert in a particular industry or you have a specific niche that you want to cater to? If you are an expert in a particular area, say fashion, then your reel should focus solely on that area of expertise. However, if you have multiple areas of expertise – maybe you're into hosting but you also are an expert at hunting – try to balance it out by making two reels. You should make a general host reel and then a specific reel for your area of expertise. These days, you need to be as specific as possible, because many of the shows that are being created have a very specific target niche or audience. Look at a show like *Pawn Stars* or *Mythbusters*. Those guys serve a very specific niche. Know what your specific expertise or niche is, and tailor your reel to reflect that.

In terms of reel production, there's some debate about whether your reel needs to look like a professional production company did it. The quick answer is no, but let me qualify that. It depends on where you are in your career and the types of jobs that you're auditioning for. If you're trying to get hosting gigs with local production companies, the quality of the reel will not matter nearly as much, but they'll still want to see your personality. Now, if you're auditioning for a national network reality pilot, they're going to want to see high quality material on a high quality reel. On this tier of the business, the high-quality reel tells them you've already worked with some high-level productions and know exactly what it takes to produce quality both on and off camera. Simply sending them material shot on your home video camera or cell phone will not get you far at this level.

If you're just starting out and don't have much broadcast material, that's OK! You just need to go out with any camera and start shooting yourself and showcasing your personality. When you go out to shoot your reel, do some co-hosting and add some man-on-the-street stuff as well. Get a friend to do this with you and have some fun! Make sure you show off your versatility while letting your personality and your point of view come through with these various clips. It will be a start to get you going in the right direction.

If you're a current host who has some solid broadcast material, you may think, "I need to put the highest quality video up front in my reel." Not necessarily. Because this business is built on personality, personality trumps production value in your demo reel. If your best personality stuff is shot in lower grade video, I would still put that ahead of higher quality video that displays less of your engaging personality.

A question that I often hear hosts ask is, "Should I put commercials or infomercials on my hosting reel?" Infomercials and commercials are referred to as "industrials" in the casting community. The short answer is no, you shouldn't include these on a host reel because most commercials involve quite a bit of acting and don't really showcase the "authentic" personality that you need to display to be a good host. As a side bar, you might want to put some of your industrial work on your reel, IF – and only IF – it shows a different fun side of your personality. Otherwise, industrials generally won't be effective in helping you get a hosting job.

Let's talk about delivery method. Do you put your reel online or send a DVD? I recommend both. In general, most casting directors want to initially see online links from sites like Vimeo and YouTube. But you also want to provide a DVD at the actual audition itself, because many times, right after auditions are over, casting directors will take a handful of DVDs up to their executives so they can review the people they liked. You want them to be able to pop in a DVD and watch you on a big TV screen. So, send the online link initially; then take a DVD copy when you go to an in-person audition.

Once an agent or casting director expresses interest in your reel, what should you do when you meet with them or talk to them on the phone? The biggest thing I want to stress here is the common theme that we have talked about throughout this book: BE YOURSELF. Look forward to having a conversation as opposed to an interview. Tell them who you are, what you do and have a realistic understanding of the types of shows that you are right for. You never want to go in and say, "I will do anything." This sounds like desperation. You're not looking for ANY job; you're seeking a SPECIFIC job. Realize what your strengths are and tell them why you are right for the show they're casting.

To review:

- A Host reel should be roughly 3 minutes in length
- Clips should be no more than 10 seconds in length
- Put your best personality stuff up front! Most agents and casting directors will only watch for 30 seconds before they make a conscious decision. They're looking for charisma, a sense of humor and authenticity.
- Include as many different types of looks as you can. Remember "looks" are not clothing or hairstyles, but activities such as interviews in the field, ad-libbing to the camera, teleprompter reading, etc.
- Production quality on your demo reel is relevant depending on the level you're at in your career. The bigger and more high profile the job, the higher the production quality needs to be.
- Don't include commercials or infomercials on a hosting reel unless they do a REALLY good job of displaying a specific part of your personality.
- Finally, if you do get a call back or interview, be yourself! Be confident in who you are, and be truthful about why you would be a great personality for their show or program.

If you're interested in hiring a professional to edit your demo reel, I highly recommend Brian Rose with Brose Productions. He is very creative, highly affordable and is in constant contact with today's casting directors and knows exactly what they're looking for. You can contact him through his website:

www.broseproductions.com

RESUME

Next, let's talk about your resume. When you hear the word "resume," most people assume that it's the same type of resume that you see on job sites like Monster or Hotjobs. That is not the case in hosting. In hosting, the resume is also called a "one sheet." Here are a couple of examples so you know what yours should look like.

(This is Game Show Host Todd Newton's resume from CMEG. com)

HOSTING		
Title	Part	Client
Worlds Wackiest Game Show Clips	Host	Travel Channel
Home Shopping Network	Host	HSN
Gameshow Marathon	Field Host	CBS
Reality Remix	Co-Host	Fox Reality
The Price Is Right Live	Host	Fremantle Media
CN8 Live New Year Celebration 2007	Host	
Made In The USA	Host	USA Networks
In Search of The Partridge Family	Host	VH1
Coming Attractions	Host	E!
Live From the Red Carpet	Co-Host	E!
E! News Live	Co-Host	E!
Performing As...	Host	Fox
Hot Ticket	Co-Host	Paramount

Whammy!	Host	GSN
Miss Universe Pageant 2001	Co-Host	
Instant Millionaire	Host	
Hollywood Showdown	Host	GSN / PAX

MISCELLANEOUS		
Title	Part	Client
The Price Is Right DVD Game	Host VO	
Press Your Luck Video Game	Host VO	
Family Feud Video Game	Host VO	
Password DVD Game	Host VO	
Match Game DVD Game	Host VO	

The resume of *Miss USA 2010* Kristen Dalton from CMEG. com

HOSTING		
Title	Part	Client
Worlds Wackiest Game Show Clips	Host	Travel Channel
Home Shopping Network	Host	HSN
Gameshow Marathon	Field Host	CBS
Reality Remix	Co-Host	Fox Reality
The Price Is Right Live	Host	Fremantle Media
CN8 Live New Year Celebration 2007	Host	
Made In The USA	Host	USA Networks
In Search of The Partridge Family	Host	VH1
Coming Attractions	Host	E!
Live From the Red Carpet	Co-Host	E!
E! News Live	Co-Host	E!

Performing As...	Host	Fox
Hot Ticket	Co-Host	Paramount
Whammy!	Host	GSN
Miss Universe Pageant 2001	Co-Host	
Instant Millionaire	Host	
Hollywood Showdown	Host	GSN / PAX

MISCELLANEOUS		
Title	Part	Client
The Price Is Right DVD Game	Host VO	
Press Your Luck Video Game	Host VO	
Family Feud Video Game	Host VO	
Password DVD Game	Host VO	
Match Game DVD Game	Host VO	

TELEVISION		
Show	Part	Client
Extra	Guest	Extra
Access Hollywood	Guest	E!
Inside Edition	Guest	NBC
CNN	Guest	CNN
Geraldo at Large	Guest	Fox
The View	Guest	ABC
Good Day New York	Guest	Fox
Fox and Friends	Guest	Fox
The Today Show	Guest	NBC
Jay Leno	Guest	NBC
Are You Smarter Than a 5th Grader	Celebrity Contestant	CMT

Minute to Win It, The Last Beauty Standing	Contestant	NBC
One Tree Hill, The Lonesome Road		CW
Segment Model/Runway coach for Sherri Sheppard	Expert	ABC

TRAINING

Instructor	Topic	Client
New York Film Academy, private acting classes		
Marki Costello's On-Going Advanced Hosting Classes		
Marki Costello's Hosting Bootcamp		
Killian's Commercial Audition Workshop		

MODELING

Title	Part	Client
100 Most Beautiful People	Featured	People
Million Dollar Money Drop	Spokesmodel	Fox
KandyWrapper swimsuits	Model	KandyWrapper
Sherri Hill Fashions	Model	Sherri Hill
Skechers "Love your Butt" campaign	Model	Skechers

HOSTING

Title	Part	Client
Stay in School PSA announcement	Host	TLN Channel 4 Wilmington
Breast Cancer PSA announcement	Host	MissUSA.com
Miss California USA 2010 pageant	Correspondent	KTLA
Miss USA 2010 Preliminary Competition	Co-Host	NBC.com
Miss USA 2010 show promo	Host	NBC.com

In the hosting world, the resume is actually quite a bit different and much more condensed. No need for big explanations about your job duties and all that jazz. Follow these examples when putting yours together. Also sites like www.becomeahost.com and www.gotcast.com have a template for you to fill out when you sign up. This will make your job of putting together a web resume very simple and only costs about $15-$20 a month to be on their site. The HOST resume should be one page and is stapled to the back of your headshot, facing out. It should be stapled in such a fashion that the resume is not loose or floppy. Your name should be in bold at the top of the resume.

Expertise – Optional but recommended

You never know what niche show will pop up that you could be perfect for, so, in the area of your resume where you list your expertise, make sure to put anything that you're even reasonably good at. Some casting agent might be looking for someone with host talent in your particular field or genre.

Crafting Your Bio

Now that you have built the first columns of your career foundation with a good demo reel and resume, let's get into how you draft a good bio about yourself. Not only do you want people to know about you, but also you want them to believe in your story and to get a good sense of your personality and style through your bio. Did you know that on average, people spend 30 percent more time on your social media "About" page than any other? It's actually one of the top five pages that people visit on anyone's page. Your bio is simply another extension of your talents. If casting directors and producers see that you can write and infuse your personality into that writing, that's just another leg up on the competition.

When most of us sit down to write a bio, we have no idea where to start. So what we do? We start looking up other people's bios and try to model ours after someone who probably isn't anything like us! But with the prominence of social media networking, your personal profile, About page, and your Linked In, Facebook and Twitter pages are where people are getting a sense of who you are. When they read about you, they're deciding, "Do I like them? Do I trust them? Is this the type of host I want to hire?" Use your bio to tell YOUR story and bring it to life! The one thing that makes any TV show great is awesome storytelling, and the principle here is no different. So, let's walk through the six steps of how to structure and tell your story and create a really great bio! FYI – While there are six steps here and you could write for days, don't write a tell-all novel on yourself! All host bios should be roughly 1 to 1 ½ pages in length, but no more!

1. <u>Start with a "hook."</u> This is where you describe who you are, what you do and who you help. You need to be really specific about who it is you're talking to here. You basically want to describe to casting directors how you can help them overcome their core need or challenge in finding a host. What is it that they're looking for, and how can your talents make their job easier? So up front be crystal clear about who you are and how you can help them. They need to understand how you're relevant to their situation or need, and how you might fit in with their show.

2. <u>Don't be afraid to be you!</u> What really impresses casting directors and people in general is when someone is not afraid to share their point of view. What's your philosophy? What do you believe in? What do you fight for? What makes you, YOU? It's crucial that you let others know who you REALLY are! Let your personality come out in your writing so that people get a sense of what you're about, what you stand for and who you are! Remember, the best hosts aren't

the ones that are just like everybody else, they're the ones who are different, unique and make others want to look at their own uniqueness and think, "It's OK to be me!"

3.   Tell us about your adventure! Everybody has a story about how they got to where they are. Where did you come from? Your answer might be funny, sad, inspiring or crazy, but it really helps people understand you and the experiences that have helped define you. Maybe it's something that happened to you when you were a kid or a mishap early in your career. Give people a sense of how you ventured into or developed the desire to be a host. What was the thing that made you say "My dream is to host"? This is the blood and guts of your bio.

4.   Adversity and Obstacles. I can guarantee that no matter who you are, you have been through some tough times to get where you are. Most of the time we want people to have sympathy for the journey we've been on and the obstacles we've overcome. It's those things that give us character and, many times, integrity. It shows that we weren't just handed everything on a silver platter and we are gifted. How many great stories have you heard that don't include overcoming some sort of adversity? Maybe you used to work a boring 9-to-5 job doing sales, or maybe you were a bartender or waiter and decided, "You know what, I can do this!" So, you took the big step to reinvent yourself as a host and become what you always dreamed about. Or maybe you're successful in what you do now and want to find a way to showcase yourself by developing your own show. People love to hear those back-stories of adversity and how you overcame it! In the '80s it was all about having the big job, big house, hot car and kick-ass wardrobe. Now, because of what America has been through for the last decade, people have a greater respect for those who have overcome the odds. Your struggle shows your character, and character will always be more

attractive than credentials. This is what people want to hear from you, so, lay it out and don't hold back!

5. <u>Legitimize yourself!</u> This is where you get to pump yourself up and brag on yourself. It's something we all unconsciously want to do because we want to people to know what we've accomplished, but we need to do it in the right way so we don't come off as arrogant. That's why you should put this section deep in your bio. If you go into the bragging phase right off the bat, you'll likely get that "Here we go" reaction from just about everybody: "Another TV host who thinks they're the greatest thing since sliced bread and that the world revolves around them." Hear me out here: You can brag; just be tactful about it. Here's how you do it. Talk about shows or events you've been featured on or formal recognition or awards you've received. If you've won an Emmy, this is the perfect place to talk about that! Maybe you've been featured on some well-known programs or shows. Tell us about that! This is where your third-party credibility and accomplishments let people know you're the real deal: You've done and been part of some cool things, and you're not just blowing sunshine up their skirt to get cast for a job. You want to people to know that you're confident in who you are, where you've been and your abilities. You want them to be able to see themselves in your story and connect with you; THEN they can understand, "Wow, this person is real and has the experience to back it up!"

6. <u>BE HUMAN!</u> Share the little details, the things that you like to do that everybody else might find weird. The things that you do because you love them. Who knows, maybe you go base-jumping several times a year to relieve stress, or you like to collect unique items and scrapbook them. Maybe you're a health and fitness addict who takes things a little over the top compared to most people. Do you have an alternate lifestyle that people would find unique? Clubs

you're in? Things you do? Share those! These are the stories and situations that make you special and unique. In the social media world we live in, people want to know those details!

To give you an example, I have included my bio for you at <u>www.</u> <u>timtialdo.com/about</u>

Headshots

People like to think that the hosting industry is more about talent than it is about looks. Truth is it's about both. So many different criteria come into play when a host is being cast for a show. Do you fit the persona? Are you the right age? Are you thin? Are you fat? Blonde? Brunette? Old? Young? Are you wild and crazy, or dry-humored and subdued? Don't get me wrong; all of that matters. But when we're talking about your headshot, you might've heard the saying, "A picture is worth a thousand words"? That couldn't be truer than in this situation. The headshot is what casting directors tend to remember you by after the audition, which is why it's so important to have the right one. It can literally make or break your career.

Getting a good headshot doesn't mean that you need to empty your bank account. It's a matter of finding a good photographer that's able to capture your best look and personality in one shot. The cost to do this tends to vary, but in my experience, you'll spend between $200 and $500 for a good headshot session.

Casting directors like to see a very natural look, so you don't want a look that's highly airbrushed and fake. Make-up is great as long as we still see the "real you." Don't cake it on like icing; let the world see who you really are! Don't worry about any skin imperfections like zits or moles – that's what editing is for. The photographer/editor will be able to clean up your skin so that it looks flawless.

When it comes to what you wear for your headshot session, this is very important. Wear a solid-colored top. Patterns, such as stripes and plaid, take the focus away from your face and onto your clothes. You want the casting director to notice you, not what you're wearing. Many times the photographer will want to see your features beforehand, considering things like hair, skin and eye color, and most of the time they will give you some good recommendations on clothing and color before you show up.

Also, a headshot is just that-- A photo of your head and shoulders. You can find great examples of headshots under the resources tab of my website, www.timtialdo.com.

Finally and most importantly, make sure your name is visible on the front of the photo, that it is spelled correctly, and that it appears as you'd want it to appear in the credits if you land the hosting gig you're auditioning for. I know this sounds like common sense stuff, but I've seen many people who rush to get the shots done and don't concentrate on the details, and they ended up spending extra money and extra time to fix errors. Do it right the first time and save yourself the stress. Also, be sure to update your photos at least once per year. It is amazing how much a person can change, whether you notice it yourself or not.

To get affordable headshot re-productions, I recommend The Argentum Photo Lab. You can find them at www.argentum.com

Chapter 6

---❖---

DEVELOPING YOUR BRAND

"Brand is the 'F' word of marketing. People swear by it, no
one quite understands its significance and everybody would
like to think they do it more often than they do"
— Mark di Soma

In society, there are periods of massive change and shifts in perspective called inflection points. Some very memorable inflection points in the last century are the invention of the automobile, the civil rights movement, the Internet and, in the television industry, the creation of reality programming. When you look back on these pivotal periods in time, we tend to think, "If I had only known about that sooner!" The truth is, we could know about it sooner, but we have to be looking in the right places. Because if you can recognize trends before they happen – or maybe event create a trend – there are extraordinary opportunities for those perceptive enough to realize their significance early on.

I say this because while this book is about how to get into the industry as it currently stands, it's also about how to recognize that the industry and everything about it is changing. According to Cisco, by the year 2015, 90% of all Internet traffic will be VIDEO! What I'm telling you is that the "trend" is already taking shape, and you must be out in front of it to really be successful. By 2015, tons of people probably will have their own shows because they have the ingenuity and knowledge to create them. While network TV is still very big for some shows, you need to recognize what is happening. Social media sites like YouTube, Skype and Facebook are quickly becoming the places where most people spend a majority of their waking life.

Just to give you an idea of how big it is becoming and how big you can become yourself, try this fact on for size. *American Idol*, one the top-rated shows on TV the past few years, brings in roughly 20 million to 25 million people on a per episode basis. The most watched telecast on the planet, the Super Bowl, is now consistently watched by over 100 million people. Now, take YouTube stars like Justine Ezarik, also known as iJustine. As I write this book, her YouTube channel has over 240 Million views and 1.3 million subscribers! That's one person who has more than double the viewers of the Super Bowl! And she does it just by being herself, being creative and having fun. Advertisers and companies are now banging on her door wanting to be part of the action because she has built herself as a BRAND. Just the other day I saw her on a commercial for a major electronics brand. When, like Justine, you build yourself as a BRAND, you give yourself the ability to connect with people.

A brand is the emotional and psychological relationship you have with your audience. Strong brands elicit emotions, and sometime physiological responses from those watching. What happens when you take the time to develop your brand before you do any real marketing is that it helps create an identity that will resonate with your audience. You'll more easily be able to develop an emotional relationship with your fans because, when it comes down to it, people don't buy into people, they buy into the emotional feeling that person gives them. It's about their gut feeling when they see and hear you. It's the reason they choose to watch you over something or someone else. Your brand is your cornerstone and the blueprint of how you want your audience to see and experience you. It will be the spark of all conversation about you and determine the position and strength of your ability to market yourself. Your brand must be authentic and it must be about you.

The concept of personal branding was introduced to the world in 1997, back when branding was primarily applied to the corporate culture ... things like big companies and products on the grocery-store shelf. Then personal branding started to filter into the entertainment world. Now everything about entertainment TV, from hosts to celebrities, looks very different. More and more people who are in front of a camera now approach their careers very differently. They are more cognizant than ever of the perceived value they deliver to their audience and fans. They've started to use the principles of branding to align what type of person they are with what they're doing on a daily basis and how they're going do it. What this new form of personal branding means is that if you want to advance your career and achieve your goals, you don't start when you get a job, you start right now, right where you are. You don't need a big network, loads of cash or an agent to get you out there; you can do it yourself! You must prepare for what's ahead, and if you don't, no one is going to feel sorry for you when the right opportunity comes along and you miss out on it because you weren't ready.

Mike Rowe who earned his chops on Discovery Channel's *Dirty Jobs* literally spells out in the intro of the show what his brand is all about. The copy reads, "*My name is Mike Rowe and this is my job. I explore the country looking for people who aren't afraid to get dirty; hard working men and women who earn an honest living doing the kinds of jobs that make civilized life possible for the rest of us. Now, get ready to get dirty.*" He knows his exact audience, which is blue collar America. He represents the rough, tough, roll-up-your-sleeves-and-get-the-work-done crowd. I personally think Mike is as good as anyone in the business at knowing who and what his brand is all about. That's why Ford and Lee Jeans signed him for seven-figure paydays! Like Mike, you too, need to know how and where to position yourself, and to ensure your brand online is in line with who you are in the real world. Be clear about who you are and what you have to offer so you can deliver your message clearly to every person watching.

So, how do you create your own personal brand? For those of you just starting to build your brand, the Internet and social media seem like easy places to gain instant visibility. But before you start building your online presence, you need to know who you are. Like conducting a great interview, it's all about asking the right questions – in this case, asking them of yourself. I've compiled a list of 15 thought-provoking questions that will help:

1. What is your personal mission in life?
2. What are your strengths?
3. What is your tagline? (Ex: McDonald's – "I'm Lovin it" or Cotton – "The Fabric of our lives")
4. What do you like to do; what activities make you lose track of time?
5. What makes you feel great about yourself?
6. What do people typically ask you to help them with?
7. What do you want to be known for?
8. Why does that matter?
9. What differentiates you from others and/or what are you saying that others aren't?
10. What makes you compelling to people; why would they want to watch you?
11. What skills, abilities and knowledge do you have that draw people to you?
12. What can you create for others?
13. What could you contribute to that would make you feel satisfied and fulfilled?
14. Can you help people solve or avoid a serious problem?
15. What would you regret not doing, being or having in your life?

Start by answering these questions. Write down as many things as you can and lay them out in front of you. It's likely that after you compile all this information you'll have a really good idea of what your personal brand looks like. If you need more help, there is a great book called "*Strengths Finder 2.0*" by a guy named Tom Rath. You can find it on Amazon. The book helps you figure out what your top personal strengths are and how you can really separate yourself from the crowd. It's totally worth your time for the insight it can give you about yourself. I highly recommend it because if you know yourself, you can grow yourself.

You must know your brand attributes – both the rational (those that make you credible) and the emotional (the personality characteristics that make you interesting and attractive to others). When you know these, you can write your personal-brand statement and post it somewhere where you will see it every day as a reminder of what you stand for.

Maureen Browne casts some of the biggest shows in the world and is somebody you're likely to run into along the way if you want to hit the big time. Here's what she had to say about branding and how important it is for an on-air personality:

"I feel like your personality is your brand. That being said, people need a leg up to get in the door, so having an expertise definitely helps. It has to be a true expertise; it can't just be because you wrote a column in your school paper. In the real world, we want you to have a certification after your name and know that it is credible information because the competition is so fierce in the expert world. Your brand is also what you're doing when there is no camera on you. If you look at someone like Ryan Seacrest, he's not swinging a hammer, he's not cooking, he's not a car dude, but yet he is a working and very successful host. His brand is just being a host and being a personality, much like Tom Bergeron and Jeff Probst. It's what you're passionate about; it's what you're doing when the camera is not rolling. If you're a foodie and you just want to go around and find out about all the interesting foods or maybe travel,

I feel like that's organic and authentic to you. Some people will come up and tell me that someone said, 'Oh you're this girl, this is what you are,' but that's not really who I am and what I like to do. Be careful; don't let somebody brand you for yourself ... YOU are it; you are the brand. It's got to be organic and the viewers can really tell if it's something you're faking versus something you're being."

As you can tell, Maureen is straightforward in what she is looking for as a casting director. She has seen it all and knows almost the second you hit the door if you are going to be a good candidate for the role she's casting. The better your personal brand is, the more you know exactly who you are and what you represent, the more confident you will be. And confidence is HUGE, as I have mentioned already.

Start Building Your Brand

Once you have figured out who you are and what you represent on an organic level, it's time to start building your brand with all the tools available to you. Scott Gerber, founder of The Young Entrepreneur Council and author of the book *"Never Get a Real Job,"* has five awesome tips on how to create and proliferate yourself as a brand:

1. **Authenticity and consistency** – Having one image and owning that image is very important. You want people to know exactly who you are and what you stand for, and that will help you deliver your message and craft it for your audience.
2. **Become a media personality** – Sure, you may eventually end up on a major network, but initially, you have tons of social media and online video tools that can help you build a following around your personal brand. There's YouTube, Facebook, Google+, Twitter and Linked In. Own those

different media channels with relevant content for your audience.

3. **Create a Moniker** – Perhaps you're a gluten-free baking queen, or maybe you're a car junkie; the key is to own something that you can be known for. It will help you with media appearances and to gain traction in the social media world.

4. **Connect your online community** – There are millions of people out there who can likely benefit from the information you provide. Seek them out on social networks and in the real world. Connect with them, engage with them and consistently offer them relevant information that you provide.

5. **Own a professional, multi-channel brand experience** – Building your personal brand means having various different channels where your personal image exists. And you want to make sure you're providing relevant information for all kinds of fans and followers based on each specific social media network or video channel. Be sure to own all the different networks with your own profile and own information and constantly update it so that you can build a personal brand that fits you.

What's awesome about social media is that new, easily accessible apps and tools have made personal branding easier, more powerful, and more efficient than ever before. Personal branding is now online, and you can see it on sites like YouTube, blogs, Facebook and Twitter—and these are ideal for hosts who are seeking to increase their visibility, demonstrate their unique abilities, and stand out from everybody else who's trying to do the same thing. We're going to talk much more in coming chapters about how to create these tools and put them to work for you.

If you're looking for a resource to help you build your brand, I highly recommend picking up a book by author Michael Hyatt. It's called, *"Platform: Get Noticed in a Noisy World."* I personally follow Michael's blog and it has helped educate me on the finer points of launching my personal brand.

Know What's Out There About You

If you're like me, when you want to know something, you Google it! It seems like if you don't show up on Google these days, you don't exist! My question for you is "how do you show up on the Internet?" If you Googled your own name right now, what kind of results would show up? Understand that how you're showing up right now will have everything to do with how your brand is perceived by anyone researching you. Whether it's an employer, a potential date, friends or co-workers, they all want to know who you are. Are you hiding any skeletons in that closet of yours? Your search results will help you build the ideal plan to showcase your value. They can also hurt you if you don't monitor and police them. Let me give you a quick personal story that I watched unfold at a lifestyle show I worked for. My co-host and I had recently been hired to start a new lifestyle show for a CBS affiliate. She was a former professional cheerleader in the NFL, and when our employer Googled her name, on the third page of the search results, there were some provocative pictures she'd taken in a photo shoot. Now these weren't nude or pornographic, but they were a little suggestive, and we were hired by a very conservative company. I remember for a couple of days, we weren't sure if they were going to keep her around or not. But she was able to contact the website administrator and get them pulled down before we ever launched the show publicly, and that likely saved the station any PR headaches. This is a perfect example of how you must know what's out there about you, and you must be proactive in making sure its stuff that you're comfortable with ANYONE seeing: your employer, your family, your parents, anyone. There might be some of you out there who are a little terrified at what you'll find. Maybe you haven't searched yourself in a while because truthfully you don't want to know. But I'm here to tell you that you need to! Here's why. If a shot at your dream job showed up in your email inbox tomorrow and the network said "*We'd like to bring you in for an audition this week, but first we're just going to run a background check and do some research on you. We'll follow up to book a time if you check out,*" how would you react? Would you feel a rush of elation and excitement because you know what they'll see – your personal brand; or would you feel a stomach-churning jolt of terror wondering what the Internet will churn up under your name? If you're in that second group, you need to be proactive. Start finding out what's out there and make sure it accurately reflects the brand that you are building. And don't just check the first page; check as many pages as come up when you search yourself.

I remember when I left news anchoring to pursue my hosting career. I turned in my resignation to my general manager at the end of my contract because I wasn't going to stay with the station any longer. There was absolutely nothing wrong with that, but one of my co-workers whom I call "the informer," blogged about it and the title of her blog was "Tim Tialdo is Outta There." Understand that we are friends and she didn't mean it in a derogatory way, but the way it came off to people reading it was that I was fired. We all know it's not a good thing to have been fired; from a brand perspective, just the suggestion that you were fired can be as bad as the reality. So, I had to ask her to take it down so it didn't show up when I was auditioning for new jobs.

Another way to find out what's out there on the Internet about you is to use a tool called the "Online ID Calculator." This tool works by going on the calculator site and filling out your personal info. It then it searches the Internet for your name and helps you make sense of your Google results. It then gives you advice on how to build a solid online identity that's aligned with your personal brand. You can also track the impact of your personal-branding efforts over time. You can measure your score right now and then try it again in six months to see what impact your efforts make.

If you'd like a link to the Online ID calculator, go to my website www.timtialdo.com/resources

Here are some other free resources you can use to track your personal brand online:

- Google Alerts: www.google.com/alerts – Set up alerts for your brands and relevant search terms.
- Monitter: www.monitter.com – Monitor real-time Twitter updates for up to three search terms.
- Twazzup: www.twazzup.com – More advanced Twitter search to identify influencers on a given topic.
- Social Mention: www.socialmention.com – Real time buzz widget like Google Alerts.
- Klout: www.klout.com – Track and identify social media influence.
- Twittercounter: www.twittercounter.com – Find Twitter users influential in certain areas.

Use More Than the Internet

The Internet is like most other technology. Just as radio didn't replace newspapers and television didn't replace radio, the Web is no substitute for building relationships in the real world. You still need to make sure people see you and meet you in person. But the Internet offers another route to enhance your brand.

In fact, you need to think about how to improve your in-person branding activities online. If, for example, you're hosting or emceeing a local event – a great personal-branding activity on its own – you need to think of ways to deliver your brand to those people once you leave. Have a table where you are handing out stuff, give away business cards or direct them to a website. The more people you connect with in person, the more viral reach you can have online.

Exercises:

1. Define who you are and what you stand for as a brand by answering the 15 questions listed earlier in this chapter.
2. Write a personal brand statement (A one-sentence description of what you stand for)
3. Google yourself and check out everything that's out there on the Internet about you. If there is something negative, try to contact the web administrator and request that it be taken down.
4. If you're doing any kind of events where people can meet you in person, start thinking of ways that they can continue the conversation with you online as a fan or follower.

Chapter 7

———— •◆• ————

PSYCHOLOGY:
THE SECRET SAUCE OF MARKETING

"Your culture is your brand"
- Tony Hsieh, CEO Zappos.com

A unique aspect of the TV hosting business is that it's one of very few industries that can honestly say, "It's all about us." Let's be honest, being recognized on the street and getting facial recognition is something that many of you who want to be hosts are seeking. But let me assure you, if that's the No. 1 driving force behind why you want to do this, you will have a very difficult road ahead of you. Let me explain why.

Marketing yourself in TV is a combination of things; it's not just one thing. A large and VERY IMPORTANT part of marketing yourself is learning to understand the perspective of your fans and followers. When you understand how they think and the lingo they use to describe things, then you can better communicate with them using THEIR language; not yours. If you want to become good at marketing yourself, you need to listen for what's behind the words your fans and followers use. You're listening for their emotional drives, fears, frustrations and what it is they want. ALL people seek to be understood; if you can communicate to them in such a way that they feel understood, you're going to have a TON of success attracting fans and followers. As an example, you could be posting content like weekly webisodes that speak to them personally, make them laugh or cover a topic that's interesting to them. You could be posting links to helpful information they didn't know was out there. For instance, why are you reading this book right now? It's likely because I'm giving you information that you've been looking for and couldn't find elsewhere. That means I'm catering to your needs. Remember, it's not about getting others to do what you want them to do; it's about giving them what they're looking for.

If you go to Ty Pennington's website or Facebook fan page, you'll see that he is always interacting with his fans. He frequently posts relevant content associated with his brand, which is home design. At least once a week, you'll see a video done by him describing how he designs a room or home and the thought process that goes into it. These are the types of things his fans see as valuable because they can take it and use it in their everyday lives.

Robert B. Cialdini, author of "The Psychology of Persuasion," says, "*One of the most potent weapons of influence around us is the rule for reciprocation. The rule says that we should try to repay, in kind, what another person has provided us.*" This alone should help you understand why helping other people get what they want will help you get what you want.

The fundamental mistake most hosts make when marketing themselves is they try to talk to people into "liking" them instead of communicating "I understand what you want and what you're trying to achieve and I'm here to help."

Hear me loud and clear when I say this, "YOU MUST STOP TALKING ABOUT HOW GREAT YOU ARE!" You must start talking to your fans about THEIR needs and what THEY hope to get out of watching and paying attention to you. If you don't, you're going to be banging your head against a wall as you try to increase your following. It isn't enough to be talented and entertaining; you have to connect with the audience on their terms. Check your ego at the door and learn from the people that matter most: your fans and followers. This is the path to success.

Even if you're already an established host with a good following, there are only two things that really matter in marketing yourself as a TV host:

1. **How You Market Yourself** – Connect with other people and show them that you have something that helps them. Social networking has been a tremendously successful way for hosts to promote themselves, but be smart about what you're putting out there. If you're a fashion expert, blog about fashion, give some great tips, post helpful and interesting articles about fashion; don't talk about your commute to work or what you had for dinner. When you talk about stupid crap, you lose followers. If you don't have a personal brand just yet, don't be afraid to have a point of view about what you're passionate about. Shoot videos. Put them on YouTube. Use your Facebook posts to let people know what you have going on and how it relates to them. But DON'T get reckless with any strong opinions you might have on any particular subject! This will certainly turn people off to your page and even cause them to stop following you.

2. **Creativity and Innovation** – You need to be creating new stuff that people want to see all the time. For the professional host, this includes new videos, blogs, webisodes, podcasts, articles and the many other forms of content. Look for content that can teach, entertain, inspire or evoke emotions like laughter or excitement. Also, don't be afraid to create your own projects. Write, direct and star in your own material and get it out there. This is what will drive the viral reach of your social media pages. By developing new and fresh content on a regular basis you're providing new reasons for your fans to pay attention to and interact with you.

Send postcards or email flyers to casting directors to alert them about your upcoming appearances. Casting directors, producers and directors all want to work with people who are working. If you are busy, you are more appealing to them.

Your most important Marketing tool as a host

Using video to market yourself as a host is something you need to integrate into your marketing plan – not only to connect with your fans, but to make yourself visible to casting directors and producers that are looking to hire for their shows. The effectiveness of video is too big to ignore, and you can't deny the results. This means you should be talking to the camera on a daily basis and welcoming your fans into your life. Here are the three reasons why video NEEDS to be integrated into your daily marketing regimen:

1. **Deeper Connection**

   Video allows for a much better, deeper connection than you can get through text or photos alone. Text and photos have their place in the industry, but video allows you to connect on a whole different level. Video is just a more effective form of communication. It's a message, wrapped with expressions and visible narration. You really don't have to concentrate to understand it; you just look, listen and react. That's why it creates such high response rates on social media. To absorb a video is absolutely effortless. Video taps into our deep, subconscious drives that have been hardwired by years of personal experience to respond within seconds to verbal and visual cues. To get scientific for a second, the amygdala—which is a cluster of almond shaped glands in the brain developed near our Neocortex produces our rational thoughts and responds to visual cues and information within FRACTIONS of a second.

   We don't think about a video because it is instinctive. Our reactions to this kind of information are so hardwired and fast, they happen before the rest of our "conscious" thought process can catch up—making them close to involuntary. This is what the entire hosting industry is entirely built around whether you knew it or not. There is no better way to connect with your audience and fans than by talking to them on camera! I can't tell you how many times I get positive comments on my video e-mails or vlogs by people who tell me they watch them consistently. While I love text e-mails, I don't get people reading them again and again; people do watch my videos again and again. Video is simply a stronger form of communication.

2. **Video helps you build your brand**

Video helps you engage, share who you are and build trust and rapport with your fans and followers. People pay attention to and follow people they like, know and trust, and nothing compares to the power of video when it comes to relationship building and engagement. Trust me when I say, someone who's doing video will automatically have more marketing power! Even big companies are starting to realize how valuable this is, and they're implementing it in their marketing. Video marketing allows your friends and fans a more intimate interaction with you, making them feel like they know you. Video also circumvents the bias or preconceived notions that can come from a still photo.

3. **Get ahead of the curve!**

You can't ignore the statistics on how powerful video is. Just look around the Internet and you'll see stats everywhere about the use of video. I mentioned earlier in the book the statistic from Cisco that says 90 percent of the Internet will be video by 2015. I use videos as a way to connect with friends and co-workers, and I love the responses I get. That being said, I realize that some people aren't fully comfortable with being on camera every day just yet. If you're one of those people who gets nervous about talking on camera, or you're afraid of how you will look, or maybe you don't feel the production value is as high as you'd like it to be … congratulations, that means you're NORMAL!

When I talk to people about why they aren't doing video to promote and market themselves, I find that one of their biggest obstacles is the "level playing field" mentality. This type of thinking stems from the fact that we all like it when things are "fair" and "just." This means we like it when we get the same treatment or results as everyone else (or just a little bit more). This is what our entire justice system is built around; it's what dictates the rulebook in all sports. It's comforting to have all the rules spelled out and for results to have a certain amount of predictability. But the hosting business is a cutthroat world. If you're playing the game with the goal of getting the same results as everyone else, you might be protecting yourself from failure, but you're also embracing "average." I'm not saying you should cheat or compromise your values to stand out in the crowd; but if you want to effectively market yourself and build a fan base, you must forget about the level playing field. The more creative and different you are with video, the stronger your marketing value. You must get outside the box of status quo thinking and open up your perspective to what's possible for you as a host. It's a necessary mindset for massive success. Developing your brand is a process, and getting it to come across on video is the most important thing. Don't let perfectionism keep you from making progress: Even if the quality of the video you're shooting when you begin is not what you'd hoped it would be, stick with it; be creative and let your personality shine. Poor production quality is a challenge, but it's a challenge that you can address and overcome; not shooting anything at all because it's not "perfect" is like giving up before you even get started.

Short-term thinking is another thing you must try to avoid. It's unfortunate that we live in a society that wants everything right now, because that's not how a successful brand or business is built. Good or bad, one video or webisode is not going to make or break your career. Your brand is built over time. When you do something that is designed to create a long-term effect, it usually doesn't look attractive in the short term. Think of a bamboo tree. It spends three years growing its roots underground. There's no growth above ground during this entire time. But after three years, all of a sudden, when the root network is established, the tree will start growing up to 3 feet per day. That's crazy growth! In the short term, though, it looked like nothing was happening. If you go back and look at the Silicon Valley boom among computer business in the mid-1990s, everyone wanted to jump in and make quick money. Today most of those companies are bankrupt and still licking their wounds from all the money they lost. The bottom line is: If you want success over the long term, you need to take consistent actions in the short term. That means no matter what the quality of your videos when you start, you must start! You can only get better and build a loyal following by taking consistent action for the long term. If you've been doing videos at least once a week for two years, I guarantee you're building a good foundation for your brand. However, if you've only been doing videos for three months and wonder where the results are, you're being shortsighted. You need to have patience and constantly be looking at ways to improve your marketing ability and presentation.

I recently had a conversation with my good friend Nikki Boyer, host of *Yahoo's Daytime in No Time*. She is one of the most successful Internet TV hosts on the web, and even though her show is completely web-based, her audience reach is stronger than many network television programs. In 2012, her show crossed the 400 million views mark. Through hosting that show she experienced the power of what the web can do in terms of marketing. But it wasn't always that way. Here's what she says it taught her about online personal branding and marketing.

"I was sort of resistant to it because I didn't like the idea of doing work that I wasn't getting paid for. I felt like I needed to find actual work that

pays; but then you realize that's the way social media is now, and the way the web is, the jobs go to the people that have done that. I think I learned it the hard way because I feel like I'm a little bit behind the curve. You go online and there are hosts and actors out there that have a crazy web following, and I wish I would have gotten focused on that a little sooner. The one thing I can encourage is to create your own brand, create your own voice and create your own following because people want to hear what you have to say no matter who you are. If you have a specific point of view and an idea about how you view the world, that's what makes your perspective unique. Whether that is creating video blogs or your own show once a week, do it; put it out there, get a following and find a way to get your voice heard. If it starts with 10 people that are loyal, then you take those 10 people and you try to build off of those."

If you have a small following and you want to grow it substantially, one of the questions you should ask yourself is, "How can I offer value?" Nikki creates value through her video blog on www.whosay.com by making viewers laugh on a daily basis. Nikki knows that her strength is being good at improv and using her facial expressions and energy to entertain others. Like Nikki, as you develop your on-camera skills and put them to work, start looking around for opportunities to create value through your videos. Remember that success is an indirect game – if you focus on creating more value, success will come. If you're just focused on making money or becoming a celebrity, success will be harder to grasp. Here are a few key things you should do on a regular basis to increase your ability to create value for your fans:

1. Timeliness: Be on time. Deliver on time. If you're not going to be on time, let people know beforehand.
2. Consistency: Deliver consistent results. Show consistent emotional stability.

3.   Quality: Do a little bit extra. Make it as good as you can. Add that little extra flare that lets people know your product is created with quality.

You've likely learned a lot in this chapter that you didn't previously know and now you must go out in the world and DO IT. By this point you've likely identified your talents and potential opportunities. Now it's about action and implementation. Studies have shown that when the most successful people come up with a good idea, they put it into action FAST. They don't think about it or procrastinate. They take action and do it. My personal experience confirms that this is true. I know many successful people, and when they get a good idea, they don't put it on a list somewhere and hope to get to it later; they go do it right then. They understand the principle that if they don't start right away, they won't build any momentum.

It's taken me a lot of years, a lot of trial and error, and a lot of talking to people more successful than I to figure out all these things. Please understand that at first it's going to be a little disconcerting to go out in the world and apply what you've learned. You might feel uncomfortable and vulnerable, but that's how it happens for all of us. If you do it and you stick with it, even as you struggle with its newness, you are accomplishing what you need to in order to get to the next level; to become the super star you know you can be. I wrote this book because I want you to turn your God-given talents into a successful career in front of the camera. It's about making you proud of your own accomplishments. It's about showcasing your greatest gifts while helping others grow and do the same. The people who look back on their struggles with pride and know that the trials and tribulations were worth it are the ones who took action, stuck it out through the tough times and never quit trying. Great success in this life never comes easy, but when you obtain success, I can assure you it is worth every bit of pain you endured along the way.

Exercises:

1. Start learning about your fans and followers and what their needs and wants are. When you find out, start catering to them by offering content that speaks to them.

2. Create Value – What are some things that you can be creating to help your audience get what they want? Is it blogs, videos, products, laughter? Sit down and make a list of things you could do, and start implementing a plan to make them happen.

3. START DOING VIDEOS! – I don't care how good or bad you think they are, the sooner you start doing them the sooner you can develop your skills … and a larger following!

Chapter 8

---·•·---

THE MARKETING TRIFECTA:
VIDEO, FACEBOOK AND YOUTUBE

*"In the long history of humankind, those who learned to
collaborate and improvise most effectively have prevailed."*
– Charles Darwin

The world we live in is more connected now than at any time in history. The days of sending letters and using a "land line' are well past us. Now smart phones, tablet computers and wi-fi connect us to video content and information anywhere, anytime, 24-7. This new generation of communication means that you must expand your knowledge and reach by embracing all the tools available. It seems like every day brings another app or tool that is the "new" way to market yourself. Rather than wade through the thousands of possibilities, I'm going to educate you strictly on the titans of social media: video marketing, Facebook and YouTube.

The statistics as I write this show that more than 800 million people are now on Facebook. That's more than double the population of the United States alone! YouTube users are uploading at a rate of 48 hours of video every minute, with nearly eight years of video content uploaded every single day! The site now has what are called "partners" who've created channels and attracted audiences that advertisers will pay to reach. We'll be talking about how to do this yourself later in this chapter.

Blogging and posting on social networks are increasingly the most common ways to communicate and market yourself, but if you're still mainly focused on posting words, you're not using the real power of online marketing to your benefit.

Social network marketing has evolved from 140 character messages to video content that draws people to you over a period of time as a trusted source of entertainment or information. People have changed in reaction to online media. Attention spans are shorter, and people literally have thousands, if not millions, of options to attract – or distract – them. To grab their attention and hold it, you have to provide awesome content. So, how do you do that?

Get Started Now!

The first step is to begin producing a video blog, or vlog, for your audience. Vlogs have an appealing affect to the people who see you and who sympathize with your content. They are a societal phenomenon and are here to stay.

First, get a video camera or a mobile phone with video capability. Ideally you want something that shoots high quality HD web videos and is compact enough to take with you wherever you want. It should also allow you to edit the material on the fly, making it quicker and easier to upload. Also, invest in a good microphone; a video in which you can't clearly hear the person speaking is annoying, not engaging. Getting a decent microphone to wear will overcome this challenge. If you are strapped for cash, however, go ahead and work with the video camera as is until you can afford a microphone.

Content of a video blog

Most people tell me they would LOVE to shoot a vlog, but they have no idea what to shoot or where to start. So, in this chapter we're going to cover the key steps for video blog production.

Visualize

What do you want your vlogs to look like? Think of filming: All films have a beginning, middle and ending. What point do you want to make? What is your demonstration? If you have no idea on how a vlog really looks, YouTube has many, many great examples. But sit down with a sheet of paper and map out what you'd like to talk about and see. With practice, you'll develop a style and flow that works best for you.

Shooting Content

In terms of what to shoot, do anything you can think of; a mixture of your humor, everyday life, struggles, successes and life's simple pleasures. You could feature anything from your favorite food to a reality show you want to talk about. You could even talk about vices, poor sleeping habits, workouts, diet, ANYTHING. Don't be glued to one style. Try different approaches and see what's working and what's not. You can use the "insights" tool for both YouTube and Facebook to find out how long your viewers are watching your videos.

The cool thing is, your vlog doesn't have to be Hollywood-produced; it just has to be the REAL you. Remember, shorter is better! If you're scripting out your material to read from a teleprompter, 150 words a minute is a general guide, depending on your read rate. According to research from YouTube, the videos that get the most views are between 2 and 8 minutes long.

The First 15 Seconds Are Crucial!

Make the beginning of your content compelling, entertaining or engrossing to viewers. Attention spans are getting shorter and shorter in our fast-paced society, so the first 15 seconds are crucial. The faster you hook the viewer, the more likely they'll watch the full length of your video. So, what about your video will convince viewers to stick around? What is the one big idea you want your audience to walk away with? Fill in the blank: I'm excited about showing this video because_____. You need to communicate this in the first 10 to 15 seconds.

- Example: The late Steve Jobs, former CEO of Apple, used to start his presentations with a "passion statement," which is a brief headline that grabbed the attention of his audience and gave them a reason to listen. Probably his most famous line was *"TODAY APPLE REINVENTS THE PHONE!"* Immediately you knew what you were going to see for the next hour, and it kept you watching. Try and do the same thing with your videos.

Tease the Viewer

In order to successfully accomplish this you should:

- Welcome your viewer
- Tell them briefly what they're going to see
- Ask a question to spark their curiosity
- Tease what's coming up in the rest of the video.

This helps the viewer answer the question "What am I watching?" You could even start with a quick clip of what's to come later in the video. Fact is, if they don't know what they're watching immediately, they're going to click away to something else.

You can definitely produce fun, flashy intros for your brand, but remember the reason people are going to keep watching is because of your personality and the content you provide. If you do a produced intro, 5 seconds is the ideal length.

Get Interactive

Keep in mind that when you're producing videos for online use, they should be as interactive as possible. When you do things like adding calls to action, it creates engagement among your viewers and increases the number of fans, subscribers or followers you have.

Calls to action should be simple. Good examples of effective calls to action would be:

- Subscribe to my channel
- Like or share my video
- Ask a question that has a yes/no or a/b type answer in which they can leave a comment

Your call to action is not the place for a passive voice. Get right to the point with plain language that makes a strong case to take action. The call to action should direct and answer what, why and when in seconds.

Place your call to action in multiple places throughout the video. Repetition reinforces what you want your subscribers to do and provides extra opportunities for those who only scan through videos.

When your call to action causes viewers to "like" you on Facebook or "favorite" you on YouTube, this increases your ranking and searchability, which increases the amount of traffic to your videos.

There is no specific section of the video where you must place your calls to action. Rather, insert them where you think they will work best based on your specific content.

Scheduling your Videos

Releasing videos on a recurring schedule provides structure to your channel or fan page that your audience or fans can rely on. If they know, for instance, that you put out new videos every Monday at noon, they'll start to look forward to and rely on that time for entertainment or information.

Also, if you're posting content that has to do with something relevant to everyday culture, use the trends in your industry or niche as landmarks to post your content around. For instance, there is a good reason that *The Today Show* has costume designers on the week of Halloween or that many networks air year-end specials around New Year's Eve.

When you produce these videos, look for relevant places to post them like blogs, websites and communities that are following the same types of stories and content. This will increase your visibility and ability to attract more viewers.

A good minimum frequency to post video content is at least once a week, but it really depends on your audience, goals and content. The general rule is the more videos you post, the higher your viewership and page ranking on YouTube.

A great way to get more supplemental video content for future vlogs or webisodes is to keep your behind-the-scenes footage and any bloopers that occur.

Upload

After loading your content into your computer, and maybe doing some editing, start posting! Keep in mind, YouTube doesn't allow videos over 15 minutes long or 2MB in size unless you sign up for an account, so if you're strapped for cash do your best to plan out your vlog and avoid rambling.

When is the right time to start? NOW! Go assemble your equipment and go for it. Record it whenever you want because anytime is the best time. Just make sure viewers end up understanding what you've recorded.

How Facebook Can Kick-Start Your Hosting Career

What's amazing about Facebook is they've given you a way to build your own personal fan site and interact with any of the other 800 million users on the site. The marketing firm Hubspot reported in 2011 that on average, 68% of adults on social networking sites are there for entertainment and 37% follow celebrities. Edison Research and Arbitron found that 80% of social media users preferred to connect with brands via Facebook. This is great news for you!

That being said, don't just go hit the "easy button" and think creating a basic fan page is going to get it done. It's merely the first step. What's awesome is that Facebook has made the very difficult process of marketing yourself into a cheap and easy solution – if you know what to look for. I'm going to walk through how to create a fan page that gets more followers and more engagement. If you're willing to put in the necessary work that goes along with that, you'll be well on your way to promoting your personal brand in a BIG new way.

Developing A Facebook Fan Page

STEP ONE - RESEARCH

In order to get a pulse on the hosting community, browse Facebook and find hosts in the business that you can learn from. Look at the pages of the big names out there that you admire. To see some of the better fan pages I've come across, go to my website: www.timtialdo.com/resources.

If you can't find a host's fan page, go to their personal website and see if there's a link to a Facebook fan page. When you find some good pages, gather information from them on what seems to work well. For instance:

- How often is the page posting?
- What times are they posting?
- What are they posting and, more importantly, what's getting the most interaction – photos, videos, links or questions? When you figure that out, don't hesitate to copy what is working!
- How many people post directly on the page? How often do they respond to a post?
- Does the page have a custom welcome tab and photo?

Also look at what isn't working for them, avoid doing the same and/or figure out a way to do it better.

STEP TWO – CREATE YOUR PAGE

To create a Facebook fan page, go to the link I've provided at www.timtialdo.com/resources and click on "Artist, Band, or Public Figure." To create a site as a TV host, there are a few different options under the "category" pull-down menu. Depending on your current career status and what your expertise is, I would recommend one of the following:

- Entertainer
- Journalist
- News Personality
- Public Figure

After you've created your page, it's time to make it look slick and sexy! Remember, it should be a warm inviting place for people to visit and should give your fans a clear picture of what you are about.

One of the best ways to do this is to add an attractive welcome tab. As of March 2012, Facebook changed the way fan pages are laid out, but the ability to have a custom "welcome tab" and "like" gate still exists.

To have a beautiful custom page, if you have a Mac you can build your own in an Iframe application. If that sounds way too complicated – like it did to me – there are several Facebook apps that can help:

INVOLVER - involver.com/applications/
This is a very easy page to use to install an attractive welcome page. Oh yeah, and since you're in the TV business and VIDEO is your No. 1 modality for delivering content, you can add a YouTube video box app from this site as well. To keep up with the highly visual theme, there's also a photo gallery and Flickr tab apps. You can even install an app to poll people. A very useful page to bookmark!

WILDFIRE – www.wildfireapp.com/
The Wildfire Iframe app is currently free and works well. It's easy to install and has fan-only content capability. You can use your own image for your Welcome page or, if you want to spruce it up, you can do HTML programming.

SHORTSTACK – www.shortstack.com/
This is another great Iframe application, and if you want more options, you can customize your Facebook page with contests, sweepstakes, videos and custom forms.

PAGEMODO – www.pagemodo.com/
This is the app I personally used when creating my Facebook-like gate. The app is very easy to use if you want to have multiple photos and don't know anything about coding apps.

FIVERR – www.fiverr.com

Hire people for 5 bucks to do things like design an attractive fan page, drive traffic to your site or even record a testimonial for you. It ALL costs $5. You pay by Pay Pal and you can track your work in progress, exchange files and communicate. Pretty fascinating stuff!

How to Build a Following

When you create a Facebook fan page, there are some best practices that can definitely help you generate more followers and interactions. Here are a few of the better ones:

- Post Every Day – Studies show that posting 3 to 5 times per day can be effective for fan pages. Also, the weekend tends to be the best time to post because that's generally when the most people are on Facebook.
- Focus on Interaction with your fans – Ask questions, post tips and link to articles or videos that your audience will like and share. IT'S NOT ABOUT YOU! When you make posts about your audience and not about you, you'll develop a much stronger and deeper relationship with them.
- Post a call to action – Ask people to "like" or comment on your posts. Also have them watch your videos or go to your website. I know this sounds like common-sense stuff, but you'll find that unless you tell people to do something, they usually don't do it! When you ask them to like, they expect something in return. According to Hubspot, 63% of users who like a page or brand expect something in return. This means things like access to exclusive content, photos, videos and interaction with the person or company running the page.
- Use the 80/20 Rule – No one likes self-glorification and they never respond to it. When posting personal videos or information vs. content/links, use the 80/20 rule. If you're posting something five times a week, make one of those

posts about your own video content or info and the other four helpful or fun content for your fans.

- <u>Make it fun!</u> – Facebook is meant to be a fun place to be! Stay true to who you are and let your personality and personal brand shine. BE YOU and have fun with them! Don't be afraid to post things that you find interesting or funny; just use good judgment if it is something questionable.

We're not all super communicators, and sometimes we just don't have the time to be posting 24/7. To start building fan engagement and community, here are seven apps that can help:

FAN OF THE WEEK - http://apps.facebook.com/fanofthe/
Add a Facebook "fan of the week" app to get more comments, posts, likes and fans. Every week, one fan out of those who interacted with your page is picked as "fan of the week." This encourages everyone to participate more. It's fully automated and picks a random fan for you. Once you install it, you don't have to do anything else, it runs itself. Easy to install and effective at generating fan page interaction!

BOOSHAKA – www.booshaka.com
This gives points to fans for posting, commenting or liking stuff on your wall. A custom tab called Top Fans will appear on your page that enables you to track all your fans' activities. A pro version also lets you allocate perks. Fans get the points for posting to your wall and they also receive points for posting likes and comments. You can view the stats of each fan listed and see how they have participated. The app also gives you a complete history of each fan's activity on your page.

NETWORKED BLOGS - http://apps.facebook.com/blognetworks
Got a blog? This lets you connect it to your Facebook page, which auto-publishes each post you write onto Facebook. Fans can like,

comment, or share directly from Facebook. Even though I will say it's always best to manually post to FB for engagement purposes, sometimes automation is very helpful when you know you're not going to be near a computer. The app puts the title of the blog post, the first picture in the post and the first few lines of the post on your Facebook page. This will allow for easy sharing of your posts by others.

POST PLANNER – www.postplanner.com

You can't be on Facebook 24/7, so use Post Planner to schedule posts there. It has the added perk of enabling you to schedule posts with pictures or video. And you can schedule your posts for specific times. The only drawback, if there is one, is that it costs $4.95 a month to do so.

CONTACT ME – www.contactme.com

Make it easy for people to get in touch with you with a contact form on your Facebook page. With the Contact Me App you can add many different fields and customize the form.

CONSTANT CONTACT – www.constantcontact.com

Many people wonder how to add a newsletter signup to their page. There are lots of ways, but what I like about the Constant Contact application is that it is very simple to use. You will have to establish an account with the Constant Contact email service. The signup doesn't allow for a lot of bells and whistles, but you can add text to talk about your newsletter and even a picture. For people who are intimidated by code and too much customizing, this application can be the way to go.

IF THIS THEN THAT – www.iftt.com

This puts the Internet to work for you. You can monitor the Internet for stories or articles on your subject area and IFTT will automatically create a status message on Facebook and can even send a text message.

Do Your Own "Live" Show On Your Page

Since you're in the business of being on-camera, the more you do it in front of others, the better you will become. And once again, your Facebook fan page allows you to do this! Live events on Facebook allow you to speak directly to your audience and vice versa. To do so, you'll need an app or plugin for video. Here are three good ones I recommend:

LIVESTREAM – www.livestream.com
USTREAM – http://www.facebook.com/ustream
LINQTO - http://www.linqto.com

Live video allows you to showcase yourself and your abilities. It also shows appreciation to your fans by giving them an experience that's unique to your personal brand and providing something they can share easily with their friends. This exponentially increases your reach – for free!

Create Your Content And Engage Your Fans

The more often you or any of your fans comment, click, like and tag content from your page, the more likely it is that your stuff will show up in their news feeds. It's called EdgeRank, and it measures your exposure on Facebook. Don't assume that people will respond just because you gave some good content. You still need to give them a call to action. This means you must ask them to respond in some way by saying things like. "What do you think?" "Do you agree?" "Vote now!" If you look at posts from successful Facebook sites, you'll see that they're always asking for some type of input in their posts. So, when you want a response from your audience, ASK FOR IT!

Advertise Yourself

One of the great advantages of working at a television station or a network in the past was that they advertised you as a brand, and that helped get your name and face out there to the masses. But as an individual, the cost to do something like that was exorbitant … until now! The dirty little secret of Facebook fan pages is that, while you can build a great audience, you never quite get to communicate with them as effectively as you'd like. So, what's the best way to get you out there to droves of new fans? Advertise on Facebook! It's not expensive and you can set your financial limits on a daily basis as high or low as you want to. You can even run the ad as long or as short of a time as you want. But the good news is, if someone clicks on your ad, that means they're interested in seeing who you are and what you have to offer. You can target people by interest and demographics and you can even put a photo on your ad that plays a major role in getting you noticed. (TIP – The Color RED has been proven to be most effective on Facebook ad photos)

An awesome new feature of Facebook advertising is that you have the ability to target people via connections. That means you can target people who are fans, who aren't fans and even people who are friends of your current fans. To set up your own advertising ad, go to:

http://www.facebook.com/business/ads/

Find Out How You're Doing

You might be doing everything just right to build a great Facebook fan base, but now it's time to confirm that's the case. To find out, you can use Facebook's analytic package called Insights. To see the Insights for your page, click the "edit page" button on the upper right-hand corner of the page. Then select "Insights" from the left-hand navigation. Click on "See Details" for interactions and it will take you to a page showing how many times each of your page posts has been viewed.

The time you invest in learning more about Facebook marketing – and marketing in general – will help you generate more traffic to your page and your personal website (if you have one), and it will provide you more and better ways to generate and interact with fans.

Create a Calendar for Your Content

Remember how we talked earlier in the chapter about scheduling your videos? The same goes for Facebook video posts. If you take the time to plan out your posting calendar, deciding what you'll post and when, this will make your life much easier. When most people hear they need to post at least once a day, and ideally three to five times a day, they get overwhelmed and think, "How am I going to come up with that much material?" Take a breath and keep reading. Using some of the above links and mapping out a calendar gives you a road map to follow. You have enough to worry about in your daily life without waking up every morning and wondering, "OK, what do I post today?"

I recommend a weekly calendar to start out. I usually sit down on a Sunday evening for about 15 minutes and plan mine out. You can mind map a calendar with apps like Mindnode. Go to www. mindnode.com. This is a very effective planning tool you can use if you have a Mac. If you have a PC, I highly recommend MindMeister for its simplicity and functionality. Go to www.mindmeister.com

This will give you a structure to your daily content for the week. You can use things like your own videos, third-party links, photos, questions, polls and a fan of the week. As an example, here's what one of my Mondays looks like:

Monday:

Morning – I post my "Life On Air with Tim Tialdo" podcast. (You can listen to it right now at my website www.timtialdo.com.)

Afternoon – I post a funny video or commercial (people love to laugh, and when you give them something to laugh about, they always remember how you made them feel).

Evening – I post a current TV host job posting or an article relevant to the industry.

As you develop your own personal calendar and plan, your fans will start to understand your patterns and look forward to many of the things you're doing.

YOUTUBE

For hosts, YouTube might be one of the greatest creations EVER because it allows you to broadcast whatever you want, whenever you want! No longer can you only step in front of a camera if you land the audition. In this modern day world of technology and simple video production, YOUTUBE is the poor man's TV network. All you need to do is create your own channel and start recording and posting!

The success of any good YouTube channel comes by laying out a well-structured plan of what you have to offer and what you want to gain. It doesn't matter what kind of personality you have, you need exposure to be seen. Your YouTube channel's popularity and success can be crucial to that.

YouTube viewership is now in the BILLIONS. Everyone has different reasons for visiting YouTube. Some people just want to brighten their day by watching funny videos or music videos. Others may want to get the latest entertainment news. No matter what you're talking about, there's someone out there on YouTube who might find your information useful. The site has generated home-grown successes that have gone on to appear on network talk shows and even make cameo appearances in movies and TV shows. YouTube has also worked wonders for many businesses advertising their services and products – and you could be their next spokesperson!

The real power of YouTube occurs in the video section of the major search engines like Google, Yahoo and Bing. When you create your title and description, use the main keyword you want to be ranked for. This will help your video's searchability rise, as will using the proper tags.

YouTube is a place for selling, and the videos can also be uploaded to other video file sharing sites like Slideshare and Flickr to increase viewership. You definitely want to share your videos on social media sites like Facebook and Twitter, which can include links to your main site.

The most important thing is to have fun with uploading your videos! People will view and comment on them, and this will help you grow and get better. It's a learning process that you can perfect in a short time. The key is when your videos DO become popular, keep them coming! An already established fan base is a very powerful tool for marketing yourself.

To help you build your YouTube channel I've compiled some important tips, best practices and strategies. By implementing these, you can help you take your channel to the next level.

If you're not a very tech-savvy person, I understand that some of this seems easier said than done, but I'm going to try and make the process of creating your very own YouTube channel as easy as possible.

Creating a Youtube Channel

I want to make sure you don't get confused right off the bat, so before you can create a channel, understand that you first must have a YouTube account. In order to do that you must have a Gmail account, so if you don't have one already, head over to Google and create one. After you've set up a Gmail address, go to YouTube.com and create an account.

Once you are signed in to YouTube, click on your name in the upper right hand corner and this will take you to your "channel." Click on "Edit Channel" in the upper left hand corner; this will allow you to change the channel info, channel design and organize your videos. To add a video, click on "Organize Videos," then click "Upload" in the upper right hand corner. When you're done making edits, click "Update Channel."

Tools to Increase Viewership

Want to get more views to your YouTube channel? This can be difficult if you're trying to use tools that get you flagged or banned. Go to www.tubetoolbox.com. It's an automated service that will drive viewers to your channel who watch videos similar to the type you're broadcasting. It's a new tool out there that is gaining traction, and I highly recommend you try it out, though there is a small cost.

Developing Your Own Personal Website

In addition to Facebook and YouTube, I often hear people ask, "Do I need to have my own personal website?" In the words of a prominent casting director:

"Yes, there is a huge value. If you're serious about your career, I think you should have a personal website to promote yourself these days."

With that in mind, there are a few ways to do this that I'll walk you through.

Personal Website

Even though creating your own website is definitely less affordable than Facebook or YouTube, if you're going to make a name for yourself in TV, this is something you'll eventually need to do.

There are a lot of different web design companies out there that offer affordable designs. But keep in mind when you're designing a web page, it can get really expensive really fast! (Decent sites usually start at about $3,000 and can go all the way up to $30,000 for the Ferrari of websites.) The good news is that your own personal page doesn't need to be super-expensive and flashy. The design should speak to your personal brand and personality, but in terms of content, it just needs to have the basics:

1. Biography
2. Resume
3. Photo Gallery
4. Reel
5. Contact Page with social media links

For links to several good personal "host" websites go to www. timtialdo.com/resources. I've provided five clean and attractive sites that don't overwhelm you with too much clutter or information.

As a caveat on those websites, there may be a few of you out there that, like me, do more than just hosting. You might do commercials, corporate videos, voiceovers, producing or emceeing. In that case, it's completely acceptable to add a few more links, but still keep the site clutter-free. Here's my own personal website as an example:

www.timtialdo.com

Website Design

When you speak to web designers about developing your site, they'll likely ask you if there are other sites you like. This helps them start the design phase. The other option is to take a little time, do your own homework and find your own website template. You can do this at www.themeforest.com. They have thousands of templates, and you'll likely be able to find a few that suit your style and brand.

Take Action Now!

While I have explained the basics to get you started in these areas, there is always more to learn as times change and society evolves. So be diligent in taking action to get your video blogging started. It doesn't have to be perfect and it certainly doesn't need to be professionally produced. The key is GET STARTED. If you come up with excuses on why you can't start, I promise you that you never will. Suck it up and show the world who you are and what you're made of! They'll thank you for it!

Exercises:

1) Create a Facebook Fan Page and YouTube channel for your content. Feel free to use the resources I provided, but even if it doesn't look like a million bucks when you begin, do it anyway. It will be the best decision you'll make.

2) Follow the producing guidelines earlier in this chapter for video blog creation. Make one and post and see what kind of response you get. Even if only a few people watch or comment, it's a start and you can grow from there.

3) If you have enough material that you feel a personal website would be the next step, read through the personal website section again and look into creating your own personal marketing site.

Chapter 9

---·•·---

WORKING WITH AN AGENT

*"Hire people who are better than you are, then leave them
to get on with it; Look for people who will aim for the
remarkable, who will not settle for the routine."*
—David Ogilvy

There are many different opinions on whether to work with an agent. Some well-known hosts were thrust into the stratosphere of success after they were "discovered" by agents. Others have struggled mightily to acquire one and have since come to despise their very existence. The right answer for you depends on several factors. In this chapter, I'll share some of my own personal experiences with agents over the years and those of others as well. But before I do, let's learn exactly what an agent is and what they can do for you.

Agents' main job is to get work for their clients. What they get in return is 10% of the compensation earned by their clients. (This is the industry average.) Agents typically facilitate auditions and general meetings for their clients, negotiate contracts and deal points, and offer general advice/guidance to their clients in regard to their careers. They typically use a less hands-on approach than managers; this allows agents to work with a higher volume of clients. The one great aspect of an agent contract is that typically, unless they get you a job, you don't have to pay them.

The one complaint I hear most often from hosts is that while some agents will go above and beyond to get them a job, other than that, they don't hear from them. This goes back to the "less hands-on approach" agents take. If you're expecting attention and guidance on a frequent basis, a manager may be something you want to look into. Personally I would only recommend managers for higher end talent working on national level shows. Every situation is different, but managers tend to be better at "holding hands" while agents tend to keep it all business.

In my own experience, I hired an agent before I ever had an on-air job in TV. I was contacted by an agent who attended the same university I did. He said I had a good reel and he was confident he could get me a job. At the time I was working at a bar as a bouncer to pay the bills, so, needless to say, I took him up on the offer. Within three weeks I had my first on-air news reporter job in Clarksburg, W.V. I was lucky that my agent only took a 7% commission because I was only making $15,000 at the time. Still, that little percentage felt like I was giving away the farm!

That same agent was also instrumental in helping me get my second job, also in news. What I found in my five years of representation is that in the beginning, he did a very good job of molding my talents and coaching me. We often did two-hour monthly coaching calls to identify areas where I could make improvements. I would send him new video of my work every few weeks and I saw measurable progress, which made writing those checks a bit easier to swallow. Once I'd been in the business for a few years, however, the calls became less and less frequent as he felt I was doing well enough to begin growing on my own. This was when writing the checks each month became harder and harder to justify. He definitely helped me get two good jobs, but I was only hearing from him every few months. There was no more coaching; merely calls to check in and see how I was doing. At the end of my contract with him, I decided not to renew and have been independent ever since.

If you're like I was at the beginning of my career – searching for work with no TV industry contacts – I would recommend at least looking into getting an agent. The upside they do offer is that they can open up doors in a way you're not able to early in your career. There are many more agents out there for news personalities than there are for hosts, but that doesn't mean you can't get one. If you're not opposed to trying your hand at news, it's a great way to get some on-camera experience in front of an established audience. In my experience of searching for a "host" agent, you need to be able to sell yourself well to land one. They're only interested in those people with the "IT Factor." If you ask them what that is, they'll tell you they can't exactly explain what IT is, but they know IT when they see IT. If you think you have the IT factor, I highly encourage you to submit your reel to them.

In terms of submitting your reel for review and possible representation, I recommend sending the agent an email with a link to your online demo. Agents typically are incredibly busy and don't have a lot of time to play around with DVDs. This is one more reason you need to get your reel up on YouTube or Vimeo where you can create a link you can send out to agents and prospective employers.

It's also important to understand that agents receive many submissions every single day; you might not hear back right away, and many of the responses might not be favorable. Given the social nature of Hollywood, any connections you might have to agents are always helpful. Friends who are actors, casting directors, and/ or producers might be able to assist you with an introduction to an agent.

To be successful in the hosting industry, I will tell you that because of today's technological advances and the ability to market yourself, having an agent is not nearly as important as it was 10 or 20 years ago. I've had great success both with and without one. The great news is there are many great shows and projects out there right now that are open to unrepresented talent. As I have shifted into hosting and taken on bigger and higher profile jobs, I'm nearly to the point where I'll need to get an agent to access some of the big-time network jobs that only agents can get you. But for those of you who aren't at the pinnacle of your career in hosting, know that it is completely acceptable and normal not to have an agent and go at it on your own.

Getting An Agent

There are literally hundreds of agencies in Los Angeles and New York. These agencies range from boutiques with just one or two agents to corporate agencies that have upwards of a hundred agents. It's helpful to find the agencies that work with the hosts you either know or have seen on-air somewhere. After you've identified the agents you'd like to contact, you can begin sending your headshot, reel and resume packets to them for review. Be sure to include any relevant press or media pertaining to work you've recently done or are currently doing.

Some host coaches offer classes, workshops and panels, and they often invite agents to evaluate their students or possibly sign them. Some call such gatherings "Industry Nights." Marki Costello does this for her students at her "Become A Host" workshops. I will say it's very helpful to keep an eye out for these types of events. They put you in good company for the opportunity to meet or speak with an agent in person. This is something you will not be able to do often.

Ultimately, it's extremely important to find an agent who believes in you and your abilities because you are entrusting your career to this person. It's important to do your research on any agent and/or manager before signing a binding contract. See who else they represent; ask their other clients for advice; ask industry contacts about their experience working with a particular agent and/or manager. By doing this, you ensure that you know what you're getting into and you won't be unpleasantly surprised down the road.

Can I Get A Job Without An Agent?

There are hundreds of hosts all over the country that have booked hosting gigs without an agent. If you don't think you've got a shot at hosting a national level show because you don't have an agent, I'm here to tell you, you're wrong. I see it happen all the time. As I've mentioned throughout this book, there are loads of hosting jobs available to you, whether you have an agent or not. This is because many production companies are going to the Internet in search of the next great personality, and in many cases, they are finding a diamond in the rough!

When I started my career in the business at *Access Hollywood*, I was told by Rob Silverstein, our executive producer at the time, that he didn't even look at talent without an agent. That was 10 years ago. My, how things have changed! While there are some jobs out there, like *Access Hollywood* or *American Idol,* for which the major networks want talent represented by a professional agent, many of the hosts on the cable networks today were discovered at cold-call auditions, on YouTube or had been recognized as an expert in another field. So, don't think lacking an agent means you can't do it. YOU CAN!

Remember, there are multiple sites out there that casting directors and producers are now browsing every day in search of the next great host. It doesn't matter if you live in L.A., NYC, or the hills of North Dakota. If you have a big personality and connect with your audience, you can land the job!

It's an unfortunate fact that some agents just have an entitled arrogance about them; like you should feel blessed to have even got through to them. I know not all agents are that way, but a few out there do give the profession a bad name. For me personally, trying to land an agent was a trial-and-error process of emailing agent after agent seeking representation. Case in point, I sent an email to a prominent L.A. host agent seeking possible representation in 2009. I'll never forget the one line email he sent back to me. I saved it so you could read it for yourself:

> *"Hi Tim,*
>   *Thanks for the submission. It is nearly impossible to represent anyone that is not LA Based. Good luck in your search."*
>
>   *Paul*

Pretty blunt and discouraging, right? As I've mentioned along the way, the TV business requires a thick skin, and this was a perfect example why. I simply knew that this man did not determine whether or not I was going to be successful. So, I kept my nose to the grindstone, and the next month I submitted my reel to a well-known L.A. production company for a network pilot they were producing. After six weeks, several auditions via Skype, and one in-person interview, I got the gig! I found that particular job on a www.gotcast.com posting. It's one of many jobs I've been in the running for via the major host job sites I've mentioned throughout this book. After getting the job, I asked the producers specifically why they chose me. One of the biggest factors was how I'd personally branded myself on job sites, my personal website and online in general.

This is why I put so much emphasis on marketing and branding yourself in previous chapters. When you're marketing and branding yourself online, you're doing what most of the agents out there are doing for their clients. If you're putting yourself in places where the casting directors and producers are constantly looking, you're bound to eventually have some success. PERCEPTION IS REALITY! What agents do is make their clients look as good as they possibly can to a prospective employer. Your job is no different. Take the time and effort to mold and create your personal brand!

The other thing to keep in mind is that you MUST be networking your ass off at all times! I have met 30 or 40 of my host friends, several casting directors and a handful of agents via the online sites and through personal introductions through another host. Much like any social media site, the online casting sites allow you to interact with other site members. I'm always out there making introductions, voting for other people's castings, complimenting their work and asking a ton of questions. As I mentioned in the beginning of the book, the hosting industry has been something of a mystery, and the only way I've been able to bring you all this information is from years of tracking it down for myself.

There are tons of ways to meet people in the business, including those mentioned above. Start trying some of these things for yourself. If you can save up a few hundred bucks once or twice a year, I highly encourage you to go out to one or two of the LA classes or workshops. They have a concentrated population of the hosting industry big wigs that can help you and you definitely want to meet them. Constantly send emails, make phone calls, shake hands with people in the industry and submit yourself for auditions. For every 100 auditions you submit for, you might hear back from 5 to 10 if you're lucky. This is a time-consuming and tedious process, but if you are committed and persistent, you will win!

Hollywood casting director Maureen Browne has this advice:

"Send us your materials ... I also find that if somebody sends those little mailer postcards every few months – of course you don't want to inundate us and constantly be in our face – but to say, 'Hey I hope you'll keep me in mind if you have something coming up on a network or show or whatever it is.' I just find that to be really helpful. I see all these kids in my class who are always going to different events and parties, and it's by meeting people and then dropping a line and saying 'I'm a huge fan of your show' that they are successful. People love it when you flatter them."

What About Local Agencies?

Agencies are a different animal than agents are, but their purpose is basically the same. So let me give you the skinny on working with an agency.

I've worked with three big city agencies over the course of my career and had a pretty good experience overall. Like agents, they tend to take 10-15% off the top for booking you for a job. This is a plus, because you don't have to spend the time going out and finding your own work. The minus is that you're also competing with everyone else that the agency might be submitting. Depending on the scope of the job, agencies can send over a handful of auditions to the client, and for others, they send over tons.

But I don't want to veer off of the "host" focus here, because much of the work you get from agencies is modeling, commercial acting or corporate video type work. Every now and then they do get calls from the networks casting for a reality show or some other type of hosting gig, but in my experience, that might be several times per year at most.

Successful Atlanta based host Lisa Ritter gave me her experience with agency representation:

"I have had agency representation for many years, and I found it to be a great help as far as educating me on what the industry is about as a whole across the board, everything from acting to modeling, even down to hosting. In Atlanta, as in many cities across the country, the challenge is that there isn't a lot of hosting work unless I'm working for a network like Fox or whatnot. That puts me back into the news arena, so it's not something I'm very interested in. Having an agency is wonderful, but in this particular field you need to have the gusto to go out and get the jobs yourself; you've got to network; you've got to search message boards; you've got to search and find the jobs so you can get the experience. It's a double-edged sword: You want to be able to work, you have to have a reel, you have to have all these tools to actually be employed, but how

do you get the jobs that actually get you a reel and get you employed?
Having an agency is great, but it is not going to guarantee you success."

Agencies are evolving though. There are new resources out there
in which large online casting agencies are networking with local
metropolitan agencies to further their reach to find new and unique
talent. If you live near a metropolitan city that has a solid agency, it
is definitely worth it to contact them and submit your work.

Submitting your materials to an agency is much the same as
it is with an agent. Most agencies have their own unique package
of what they like to see. Headshots, resumes and reels usually
encompass what you'll submit. If you're someone who doesn't have
those things, yet have what they're looking for, agencies are really
good about connecting you with people near you who do good
work for a reasonable price.

What to Do Now?

If you're contemplating whether to seek out an agent or agency,
let's review the things you need to keep in mind when making that
decision.

1. What stage of your career are you at? If you are just starting
   out in your career and don't know many people in the
   industry, you may want to look into getting a news agent
   and trying journalism to get your feet wet. If that's not
   something that interests you, feel free to send your demo
   reel into a host agent or talent agency, but make sure it has,
   above all things, confidence and energy.
2. If you don't like paying other people to do things that you
   know you can do on your own, an agent/agency might not
   be the right choice for you. However, if you need some
   coaching to continue to grow your skills and don't mind
   sacrificing some of your pay to do that, then you can either

go through an agent or fly out to either coast for some coaching classes. You have to weigh the options to see what best fits your particular budget.

3. A "news" agent and a "host" agent tend to be very different. They are looking for two completely different types of people and also have very different personal networks. I had a "news" agent that was very successful at getting me news jobs, but once I told him I was making the transition to entertainment, he was a fish out of water trying to find a pond. If hosting is all you want to do, get a host agent or make a run at it on your own.

4. Where are you located? As you saw in this chapter, some agents believe that you must live in a certain geographical zip code to succeed. First of all, don't believe that crap for a second. The industry is evolving, and they will eventually figure that out the hard way. Find an agent that's interested in "talent" and not the distance you live from a particular zip code. If that's part of their requirements for representation, that's their loss, not yours. With online video resources like YouTube and Skype, your home is now also your office/ studio, and it's visible from anywhere on the planet! The old tales that "you need to pack your bags and head west to make it big" are not the case anymore. Technology has changed the game and you must evolve and grow with it. If you do, you can be a successful host!!

Chapter 10

---·•·---

THE AUDITION

*After hundreds of auditions and nothing, you're sitting home
and wondering, 'What am I doing?' – Demi Lovato*

Y ou walk in to the room, your heart is racing, you're wondering,
"What are they thinking?" They tell you to go, and just as
you begin to start, sweat dripping from your brow, your mind goes
blank! If this nightmare sounds familiar, don't feel bad. You're not
alone. Audition anxiety is probably one of the biggest fears about
the hosting industry in general. Stepping in front of a panel of
experts who are ready to either make or break your future can be an
intimidating experience, to say the least.

The great news is it doesn't have to be that way! There are a
variety of things you can do prior to an audition that will help
you not only calm your nerves, but also stay focused and deliver a
top-notch performance. We'll go over them in this chapter.

In your career, you're likely in one of two situations. You're
already auditioning for jobs, or you're a newbie to the business and
just want to learn how to audition without completely embarrassing
yourself. Either way, I completely understand. I've been in both
situations, and I want to help. First of all, you need to understand
that there are many different types of auditions for acting,
commercials, spokespersons and, of course, hosting. But sometimes

the lines between them get blurred. People who audition in one of the other industries, like acting, can end up giving detrimental advice to someone going to a HOST audition. While there are different nuances to each, I'm going to walk you through the entire audition process for HOSTING specifically.

The 2 Types of Host Auditions

There are two types of auditions that you'll likely go through when trying to land a TV host gig. First is the video audition, where a casting director asks you to either send a link or DVD of your reel or record something specific and send it in. Second is the in-person studio audition. Most likely, if you're going to get the job, you'll have to go through both. That being said, I've never met a casting director that would fully commit to hiring someone without meeting them in person first. But you could get a job without the in-person audition, and here's proof it is possible. It's a great story I was told by a former executive at Merv Griffin Entertainment that happened back in 1994.

In that year, Merv was casting for a new children's show called *Click*. An executive said when Merv saw a reel from this young 20-year-old kid named Ryan Seacrest, he yelled "That's the guy I want!" Merv Griffin was quoted in *The New York Times* saying, "Seacrest's energy just baffled me. I couldn't keep up with him. ... He had this spiky haircut, and we knew all the little girls in the audience would love him, and they did."

I understand that not everyone is a Ryan Seacrest, but he's proof that even in a video audition, if you have a great sense of confidence and unspeakable energy, you have the potential to land a job and be the next great host!

I've had many people in the industry ask, "Why does Ryan Seacrest do so well as a host and make millions more than everyone else?" Here's why: Because he's PASSIONATE about the shows he's on and BELIEVES in what they're about. When you start browsing through all the auditions out there, the first question you need to ask yourself is WHY are you auditioning for a particular job? The people who tend to blow it in the auditioning process are the ones who never should've been there in the first place. The reasons behind their poor performance generally fall into three categories:

1. The show concept wasn't something they had a great interest in;
2. They just needed the money; or, my favorite
3. They go to every audition because "they just want to be on TV."

Understand that TV is no different from any other job in that you need to do your research, you need to understand what you're walking into, and you need to be prepared. If it's not a show you could see yourself doing, I recommend that you don't bother going to the audition; you'll waste everyone's time including your own. I'm not saying that to deter you from auditioning in general; I'm saying it so you can focus your efforts on things that serve your success. Casting directors often see hundreds of people in a day; if you don't have the passion and respect to be prepared and fully engaged in that audition, then wait for one in which you do. It will make everyone's life easier.

The Do's of the Auditioning Process

While there are hundreds of casting directors out there, they all have their own likes and dislikes. I'm going to list for you the audition DO's that seem to be universal for most of them. I assure you that if you follow these tips, you will greatly increase your chances of succeeding in the auditioning process.

Understand that Casting Directors Want you to Get The Job!

If you are one of the many people out there that gets completely stressed out come audition time, know that **CASTING DIRECTORS WANT YOU TO BE THE ONE!** If every host out there knew just how much they want you to succeed, audition nerves would all but vanish. So many hosts stress out about not being what the casting director wants. Remember, they called you in! They want you to get the job! They're not out to knock you down and make you feel bad about yourself. More than anything, they want the right person to walk through that door and knock their socks off, because when you do get the job, guess what? Their job for the day is done! They get to go home and stop stressing about finding the next host of their show. So, when you walk in there, know that they WANT you to be great and are CHEERING for you to be great. Your job is to make them happy by doing what you do best.

Get Yourself Mentally Prepared

The process of auditioning begins before you ever leave your home. I've seen so many people, especially women, psych themselves out by saying things like, "All the girls are going to be good-looking, why would they ever pick me?" While in some cases there are advantages to being a "good-looking" person, the one thing I've noticed over the years is that having a certain "look" has become less important. With the prominence of reality shows, more casting directors and producers are now focused on finding the "right" person for the job instead of relying on looks alone. What makes a particular host the "right" person is determined on a case-by-case basis depending on which show they're casting for, but as far as having their mind made up when you walk through the door, that's rarely the case anymore.

Take Time to Determine What to Wear

There are many different schools of thought about this. Some people think, "I need to wear a costume." Casting directors are looking for you to indicate how you think the host should look for this particular segment or show. It helps them see you in the role and get a feel for how it might look on the air. Don't go overboard, but show them how you think. Remember: your appearance is part of who you are. If you're disheveled and sloppy, that doesn't give a very good first impression unless you're auditioning as the host of a new show about garbage men. If you put some thought into what you wear and be creative, it will pay off. No one says you have to go out and buy new outfits. Just do the best with what you have. They are not, and I repeat NOT judging you on how expensive and up to date your wardrobe is.

Be Prepared

You must learn how to prepare yourself when going into an audition. It's very common to come out of an audition feeling like you were treated poorly. This is where having a "thick skin" comes into play. Remember, in many cases casting directors are seeing several hundred people in a day, and you are just a number. The interaction may be something like: "Hi. Your name? OK, go!" No chitchat or small talk. If you think you're going to schmooze them beforehand and win them over with your conversation, think again.

When someone calls you to book an audition, you need to know who it is you are auditioning for. Find out everyone that will be in the room. It's a good idea to keep a Rolodex of all the people you've met in this business, because it's a small business and this will serve you well along the way. Take notes when you go to the audition. Whom did you meet? Did they like you? What type of person were they? What did you do right and wrong? Follow up and network with them.

You also need to be focused on what you are auditioning for. What level of audition is this? Is it single camera, three-camera, green screen? There are general meetings, callbacks, studio tests and chemistry reads. Know what you're going in for! Do your research beforehand. With the Internet, there is no excuse not to do as much research as you can. Many times you'll be auditioning for a pilot, so nothing will exist on it yet. In this case look up the creators of the show and try to understand the type of tone they create with their other shows.

Professionalism

How you respond, interact, email, contact and engage with people says a lot about how you'll be on set. If you can continue to expand your skills, thoughts and experiences, you become a vast resource of energy that people want to interact with. Some casting directors still respond to the occasional postcard or direct mailing to fill them in on what you've been up to in the industry. They also may attend showcases and workshops whenever time permits. If you have your own website or Facebook page, they also like to check them out and see what you've been doing lately.

Bring Your Headshot, Resume and Reel

Unless you're Ryan Seacrest, Mike Rowe or Nancy O'Dell, bring these three things without question! Don't think that your agent sent them ahead of time or that they already have it or that their assistant got it to them. As we talked about early in the book, these are your calling cards; they are the most important things you can bring besides yourself. Being current with these three things, and also having them registered on the casting websites, helps out in a big way! Often casting directors will do searches on these sites before ever releasing an audition notice. There is no excuse not to have them. Put a kit together in your car of headshots, resumes and a DVD of your demo reel. Even though you may have an online link to it, it always helps to have it right there so they can see it immediately if needed.

You are Auditioning the Moment You Hit the Door!

Don't blow your audition before it even starts. Don't be disheveled and unorganized and a HOT MESS when you walk through the door. Be calm, cool, collected and, most importantly, professional! ALL casting directors will tell you that one of, if not the most important factors they remember about someone from the audition is their professionalism. Don't be complaining about the parking or why you were late. Also, DON'T MAKE EXCUSES if you haven't read the copy, or your headshot or resume isn't up-to-date. It's your job to take care of that beforehand, and they don't want to hear about it! Complaints and excuses give the first impression that you're someone they don't want to deal with.

Check In and Be Nice to the Casting Assistant

This is important because the casting assistant is the eyes and ears of the casting director. If you show up and you're making a mess with all your papers OR you are verbally abusive to the assistant, guess who's going to hear about it? After that, the likelihood of your coming back is not good. It's also a good idea to check in with the assistant to make sure you have the most up-to-date script. Many times the script is updated daily, and you want to make sure that the one the casting director has that day is the same one you're reading. Trust me, you don't want to be in the casting room when you figure out you've got the wrong script! Points will be deducted immediately! Some casting directors will be nice and let you go back out and review; others will not. Don't take that chance!

Prepare Yourself Before You Walk into the Audition

Don't ask the casting director if you can take a moment to get into your ZONE. You have to believe what you're reading, otherwise no one else will. Don't rely on "3, 2, 1, Go!" to get into the relaxed state you need to be in before going on camera. Get in that state 5 minutes before and be completely immersed in the host copy well before you go in. This will result in success.

Breathe

Many people go into an audition all nervous, which affects their breathing. They basically hold their breath, and then they try to knock out all the copy in a single breath. When you walk in, take a deep breath, in through the nose, out through the mouth. This will help in a couple of ways. It will pace your delivery better so the words don't come out at 100 mph. It also gives you oxygen, which gives you some clarity right before you start. So remember, BREATHE and take it nice and easy. Even if you have a crazy, excitable personality, reading 100 miles an hour and just getting through the copy isn't going to impress anyone.

Be in the Moment!

I heard about a story where a woman walked into an audition and said "Gosh, I hope I get this job!"

"Why?" the casting director asked her.

"Then I can pay off my credit card bills and make my rent payment!" she replied.

What she was basically telling the casting director was she was thinking about other things and wasn't truly IN THE MOMENT! When someone goes in present and prepared, even if your persona isn't in line with what they're looking for, at least they can see the prep and homework was done. If you're truly in the moment, you'll be able to adapt to any adjustments they give you. At that point, even if you don't get the job, you still had a very successful audition.

Should You Shake Hands?

I've heard a lot of people ask this question, so let me answer it from the casting director's point of view. If there are more than two or three people in the room, you don't have to go around and shake everyone's hand. In most auditions these days, there isn't a lot of hand shaking going on. Casting directors see massive numbers of people every day. Many times their biggest concern is not getting sick from all the germs they could come in contact with. So, don't take it personally if you don't get the handshake part to happen. It also could be possible they're a bit sick and don't want to give it to you. The only way to really get this part right is to follow the casting director's lead. If they extend their arm to shake hands, go ahead; if not, get ready to audition!

Make A Fan of the Casting Director!

Casting directors take detailed notes on each audition, so even if you don't happen to be the right person for that particular job, they're still going to remember you if you impress them. Also, remember the names of the casting directors. Take a mental note when you're introducing yourself. Every show and every casting team is different; however, what impresses a majority of them is someone who can back up what they're saying. If you tell them you're the "craziest person" among your friends, give them specific examples of things you've done that will support your claim. Also, what impresses casting directors is someone who has confidence; never underestimate it. You should be focused on impressing them with what YOU bring to the table, because the goal isn't just to get a particular job; it's more about making a good impression on the people you're meeting. If you do, then when a gig comes up that they feel you're right for, you can guarantee they'll be calling you back for another audition.

The Don'ts of the Auditioning Process

You need to remember that being cast on a television show also means representing a brand, a network and the show itself, so it's important to remain professional while still showing the casting director your personality. So, let's go over the things that casting directors dislike. What I've found from the many auditions that I've been to is that everyone has an opinion of what casting directors want to see. If you begin to listen to everyone else's opinion, you'll be so loaded up with conflicting information you won't know what direction to go! The following information has been gathered from some of the most prominent casting directors in the hosting business. This isn't hearsay or my personal opinion; its real tangible advice you need to pay attention to.

Don't Be Impatient

Be ready to show up on time and be ready to wait. Being impatient while waiting to see the casting director is a HUGE mistake. Everyone in the office usually works for the casting director. If you think the casting assistant or receptionist won't tell the casting director about your rude behavior, you're wrong. Be courteous, kind, polite and sincere. That will improve your chances every time. Also, be aware that delays happen. Sometimes even casting directors, traditionally very organized, can't control everything. Sometimes the cameraperson or the prompter operator or someone on the crew shows up late. This is unfortunate for everyone, but it's something you must deal with. If you get impatient and lose your cool, you'll blow your audition. You need to figure out what you need to do to stay in the moment and be ready, whether you end up waiting 5 minutes or 3 hours. Wear some headphones or stand up and walk around. Also, be respectful of the material you're getting ready to read. Don't badmouth other people or the script to somebody else. You never know to whom you might be talking!

Don't Wing It

Don't ever think that you're good enough that you can just go in and wing an audition. Practice your copy and know it well. When you edit or stop yourself halfway through a take and ask to do it again, that shows you aren't prepared. If you mess up a word or sentence, KEEP GOING! Don't stop and say, "I have to do that again!" If they want you to, they will tell you to. What they're more concerned about is the flow and personality of the audition, not whether you nail every single word perfectly and articulately. Remember, this is HOSTING, they're just seeing who you are and how your personality flows on camera. If you can navigate smoothly through the bumps, you're only going to impress them that much more!

Pay Attention

When casting directors give direction, listen! When they say, "Stick to copy" they mean, "Stick to copy!" And the audition is not the time to try to chat up the casting directors. Follow their lead. If they engage you in conversation, fine, but if they're rushing you out of the room, then pay attention!

Don't Show up Unprepared

Not being prepared is the biggest mistake any host can make. It's simply unacceptable if you are serious about your career. I have many people ask me if I ever get nervous when I'm on camera. The answer I always give is that I only get nervous when I am not prepared. Hosting is a game of confidence and preparation. If you master both, you'll succeed at the highest level. The first impression you give is a lasting impression. MAKE IT COUNT!

Don't be Cocky or Rude

As a host, you are a product, and your job is to sell yourself to casting directors and talent executives to get hired. Finding a nice balance between selling yourself and overselling is the key. If you come in with too much swagger and act arrogant, this not only ruins your audition, but also scars your future chances of getting others. I can't begin to tell you how many times I've been to auditions and watched some cocky other guy trying to sabotage others. Let me be very clear with you: If you approach it like that, you'll earn a bad name industrywide very quickly. How you treat others is a BIG contributing factor to your success ... or lack thereof.

There will always be people out there that struggle with the audition, but my hope is, after reading this chapter, you won't be one of them. Take the time to practice these tips and work them into your preparation for an audition. Once you master them, you'll find that your chances of landing a gig will increase exponentially!

Exercises:

1. Go back through this chapter and make a checklist of all the things you need to do before going to an audition.
2. On a note card that can fit in your pocket, make a small cheat sheet with tips from this chapter that you can take with you to auditions. When you get to an audition, many times there is a lot of commotion that can disrupt your focus. By pulling out this card and reminding yourself what you need to be doing, you'll stay in that zone.
3. Implement all these strategies as your audition arsenal for a flawless performance!

Conclusion

———•———

SO NOW WHAT?

"In any moment of decision, the best thing you can do is the right thing. The next best thing is the wrong thing and the worst thing you can do is nothing."
- Theodore Roosevelt

The Meatloaf Metaphor

A mother is making meatloaf with her teenage daughter, a ritual they've been doing together for years. As part of the tradition, they cut the end off one side of the meatloaf before putting it in the oven. One day, the teen asks, "mom, why do we cut the meatloaf before we put it in the oven?"

Taken by surprise, the mom began to think. She had no good reason, other than that's how her own mother made meatloaf. Together, the two called up Grandma to find the answer. After a brief laugh, the grandmother admitted she didn't know the answer either; she'd learned the technique from her mother. Their curiosity sparked, the three went to visit Great-grandma in the nursing home where she lived. Upon hearing the question, the 98-year-old great-grandmother roared with laughter. "I have no idea why you are cutting the end off the meatloaf! I used to do it because I didn't have a big enough pan!"

I use the meatloaf metaphor to define an out-of-date tradition or belief that may have made sense in the past but is no longer relevant. Unfortunately most people are busy making the same old meatloaf. Use this story to remind you to question the status quo and to challenge long-standing traditions that TV hosting can only be done a handful of ways. There are people out there everyday creating new and innovative, styles, techniques and personas that the world is falling in love with. You can be next! By awakening your curiosity, you'll be amazed at what you may discover.

Be Different!

If you're unwilling to be different, you'll never get to the next level. The very fact that the entire hosting industry does something in a particular way is a great reason to explore the exact opposite approach.

Those who will win in the future will perform more like Apple has. They are constantly reinventing themselves and seeking fresh, new approaches. If you do the same, you'll tap into the new currency for success. Your ability to improvise and take great pride in risk taking and originality will determine how well you succeed in this increasingly creative industry.

Take this example as an analogy to your career: No matter your sex, height or bone structure, if you hit the gym and start pumping iron, you'll develop bigger, stronger muscles. Being creative is no different. According to Harvard Business Professor Clayton Christensen, "Studies have shown that creativity is close to 80% learned and acquired." Practice creativity each day. Imagine how much more effective you will be as a host with that kind of creative development!

Look for ways to improve. The great thing about hard work and success is that it becomes an addiction. Just like a smoker who can't get enough nicotine in their system to keep a constant high, the human mind rewards success by never being satisfied. Once your mind is expanded with an idea or concept, it does not want to go back to where it was. So that leaves you with only one direction to go … up! Look to mentors, your successful friends, co-workers, family members, etc. to help you set your goals and become everything you've ever dreamed of being!

Time to Take Action!

I hope that this book has provided you with some valuable knowledge and information about the hosting industry. I can tell you that you're about to embark on an incredibly exciting journey that will be unique for each one of you. The experiences you'll have, the people you meet and the excitement that comes with it are honestly indescribable. But you must take the knowledge you've learned and begin applying it right now!

To begin the process I've included an action plan below. These are some of the inexpensive things you can do to put yourself in the drivers' seat of your hosting career.

- Invest in a quality video camera. You can get a good quality camera ideal for video blogging for around $100 to $150. If you have some extra funds, get some lights and a microphone to up the quality of your presentation.
- Get a DEMO REEL! Without one you are NOT a host! If you have some material already on tape or online, pay a qualified editor to put it together for you. (Go back to Chapter 2 for my recommendations.) If you don't have any professional material just yet, get out a home camera or a flip cam and have a family member or friend record you. If you don't have a camera of any kind, find someone you can borrow one from for an afternoon. Don't give up!
- Create a FACEBOOK FAN PAGE! It costs absolutely nothing and gives you the incredible ability to begin marketing and branding yourself to the world. When you

get it set up, begin doing weekly, even daily webisodes and posting content for your growing fan base. Facebook provides a ton of great information and free resources to help you so take advantage of that.

- Sign Up for the HOST JOB SITES! www.gotcast.com and www.becomeahost.com are my personal recommendations. Once you're a member, begin searching the sites for information, auditions and begin networking with other hosts and the casting directors that browse the site. Their information is usually available on the right hand side of the job board page.

- Search for LOCAL hosting jobs! Depending on where you're from, many local production companies will post jobs on Craigslist. Also, find out who all the local production companies are and email or call to introduce yourself. Ask them if you could send them a reel to be part of their Rolodex of potential talent. I assure you they are always looking for a variety of talent.

- Bookmark my site and subscribe to my RSS feed at www. timtialdo.com. I'll be posting all kinds of relevant and useful content to help you pull the curtains back on this industry and learn from those who've been doing it for years!

- START SUBMITTING YOURSELF FOR AUDITIONS! Surprisingly this is the one step that many people fail to take because they either feel like they don't have shot in hell, or they're just scared to put themselves out there for the world to see. YOU MUST start getting used to the audition process. You will not get the job a majority of the time, but for every job that you try for and don't get it, you're one step closer to the job you will land. You never know what a casting director or production company is looking for, so put yourself out there and see what happens! The worst thing that can happen is you don't get a call back. Besides, it's FREE!!

You have been led to read this book for a reason. If you are reading this sentence right now, that means you made it through the entire book and obviously have a great interest in succeeding. Before you put this book down, I want to tell you something. You have what it takes to make it as a host. You are talented, determined and persistent, and no one can stop you from getting what you want if you put your mind to it. Begin as soon as you put this book down. Prove to yourself and to the world that you are the next great-undiscovered talent! I wish you the best on this journey. May God bless your path and guide you to great success!

BONUS!!

To meet Tim online, go to www.timtialdo.com where you can also receive a free eBook and training videos to help guide you on your path.

Made in the USA
Middletown, DE
29 October 2015